D0077089

Recent Titles from Quorum Books

VENTURING ABROAD

VENTURING
ABROAD
INNOVATION BY
U.S. MULTINATIONALS

Frank Clayton Schuller

Q

QUORUM BOOKS
New York • Westport, Connecticut • London

To Robert B. Stobaugh, a friend and mentor

Library of Congress Cataloging-in-Publication Data

Schuller, Frank C.
  Venturing abroad : innovation by U.S. multinationals / Frank
  Clayton Schuller.
    p. cm.
  Includes bibliographies and index.
  ISBN 0–89930–129–0 (lib bdg. : alk. paper)
    1. International business enterprises—United States—Management.
  2. Inventions—United States—Management.   I. Title.
  HD2785.S397   1988
  658.1′8—dc19   87–37574

British Library Cataloguing in Publication Data is available.

Library of Congress Catalog Card Number: 87–37574
ISBN: 0–89930–129–0

First published in 1988 by Quorum Books

Greenwood Press, Inc.
88 Post Road West, Westport, Connecticut   06881

Printed in the United States of America

∞™

The paper used in this book complies with the
Permanent Paper Standard issued by the National
Information Standards Organization (Z39.48–1984).

10 9 8 7 6 5 4 3 2 1

Contents

Tables

Acknowledgments

After finishing the final footnotes and having re-read this manuscript for the last time, I realize how diminimous, my part, as author really is. Many have contributed to my manuscripts in essential ways in the past as they have done so tirelessly for this book. For all their help I am deeply grateful.

In particular, the faculty and students of the Amos Tuck School of Business at Dartmouth College have provided a multitude of opportunities and insights that have inspired my thinking about entrepreneurship. I appreciate the faith of Dean Colin C. Blaydon in taking the risk of inviting me to Tuck and the continued support of Dean Gert Assmuss in bolstering my spirits during my first two years of inexperience in teaching entrepreneurship. I am grateful for the insights and wisdom of Professor James Brian Quinn, who generously surrendered his well-nurtured entrepreneurship course to me, and to Professor Dennis Logue, whose knowledge of entrepreneurship and international business, was invaluable in merging two disciplines. Other Tuck faculty members, perhaps, unknown to them, have served as touchstones for various ideas. Among them are Professors Paul Argenti, Jonathan Baker, Richard Bower, Vijay Govindarajan, Thomas Selling, John Shank, Clyde Stickney, Avant Sundaram, and Ram Willner.

Many others have worked diligently in assisting me with the preparation of this manuscript. Though I have often been silent in my appreciation, I am extremely grateful for their tireless efforts: To Peter Heron, a long suffering friend with whom I have argued and wrangled over his unusually perspicacious editoral comments; to Muriel Drysdale, and her late husband Cliff, who processed various drafts almost instantaneously and proof-read them at all hours of the night; to Richard Copperstein, a friend who searched after seemingly endless obscure references and collated reams of data; to Nancy Gunn Harsha, who meticulously edited page-proofs and patiently accepted my last-minute changes.

I appreciate my family, Katie and Clayton, who have suffered through yet another "ordeal", patiently and lovingly, as always.

Frank Clayton Schuller

PART I

1

Introduction

U.S. multinationals, which in the two decades after World War II were indisputably at the technological vanguard in many world markets, have found themselves in recent years engaged in head-to-head competition for market share with both national (or local) and non–U.S. multinational firms. The last decade or so has seen national economies improving in Europe, Asia, and less-developed areas of the world, the skill of local labor forces rising, and the affluence of their populations increasing. National and non–U.S. multinational firms finally are achieving parity—or better—with U.S. technological expertise in product development and manufacturing processes. Also contributing to U.S. multinationals' loss of market shares abroad is continued reliance on outdated approaches in managing for the future.

Reactions have taken three forms. First, some U.S. multinationals, particularly those with only a modest direct stake in markets abroad, cut back or exited those markets altogether. The second and by far more pervasive tactic saw a continuation of past strategies, to wit, the transfer of domestically developed technologies and incremental improvements of existing products to threatened foreign markets. This strategy is reactive or defensive in nature, and its core motivation derives from desire to protect existing market shares. This might be regarded as a "sufficient" response, in the sense that playing the role of "catch-up guy," "follower," or "imitator" tends to maintain existing levels of sales, although by no means is this in-evitable. Innovations are incremental, frequently imitative, and derivative of domestic research and development (R&D) efforts, although some may be geared to capturing or creating new market niches. Radical or breakthrough innovations are rare, and products are neither designed nor developed specif-ically for foreign markets.

It is the third reaction with which this book is primarily concerned. With gradual but increasing frequency, a number of U.S. multinationals are moving more toward instituting a proactive strategy in innovating abroad. These U.S. firms are choosing to respond to competitive pressures by infusing their overseas subsidiaries with entrepreneurial spirit once reserved exclusively for U.S. markets, and currently evidenced by the rapid appearance of a plethora of small, start-up entrepreneur-ial firms here in the United States. Further, they rely upon these subsidiaries to identify, to direct, and—increasingly—both to research and develop innovations addressed to meet the specific needs and demand opportunities of the markets they serve. As the successful vanguards of this more proactive strategy, their experience offers a wealth of lessons applicable to other U.S. multinationals that are considering whether or not to trek down the same road. This book focuses its attention upon this group of large, wealthy, and pioneering U.S. multi-nationals; the analysis is not claimed to be applicable to smaller companies, although some lessons may bridge both groups. This reaction draws its viability from a host of factors, not the least of which is the fact that the spirit of entrepreneurship is currently "alive and kicking" in the United States, particularly as evidenced by the success of small, start-up entrepreneurial firms.

U.S. multinationals did not initiate this proactive strategy for innovating abroad; rather, its practicality and success first was demonstrated by non–U.S. multinationals, particularly those from Western Europe and, to a lesser degree, Japan. A few quick examples illustrate: Ciba-Geigy, a Switzerland-based multinational, engages in rigorous R&D not in Zurich but in North Carolina for new products to be sold in U.S. markets; Ericson, a Swedish firm, developed a telephone system specif-ically designed for the population densities, geographical anomalies, and communications needs of Australia, where it met with great success. Toshiba, the giant Japanese multinational, is developing new products geared specifically for sale to U.S. consumers. The point of these examples is that these endeavors have demonstrated through their diversity and originality of approaches that innovation does not have to hover, like a moth to a flame, around domestic corporate headquarters and around traditional domestic markets. To the contrary, expanding fully staffed and equipped R&D and manufacturing facilities overseas is one of several strategic moves that is an absolute precondition to innovating successfully abroad.

As increasing numbers of U.S. multinationals venture down this same path, which will succeed and which will fail in the long run is impossible to foretell. Innovation abroad is an evolutionary process, in the sense that innovating subsidiaries all encounter and all must respond flexibly to a dramatic series of new conditions, uncertainties, and crises that managers of U.S. firms have never before encountered. Each firm will experience these traumas differently, and vast unforeseeable disruptions in global economic and market conditions may arise to throw all bets off. The best one can offer are general guidelines, which individual firms then must apply to their specific circumstances.

Non–U.S. multinationals and national firms have taken the lead in successfully innovating for markets abroad. This fact, coupled with the proven success of small entrepreneurial firms in out-innovating large, traditionally structured corporations here in the United States, adds persuasive weight to the contention that the old ways of doing business, even if presently sufficient, may become less and less so. To this fact must be added the fact that U.S. multinationals now face unparalleled competition in markets abroad. Economies of scale in R&D and manufacturing processes, marketing power, and access to ample capital are no longer the exclusive purview of U.S. multinationals, nor are these advantages still so crucial to success as they once were. Barriers to entry for non–U.S. firms are crumbling in a wide variety of world and local markets. The rapid rise of international venture capital companies, exponential improvements in the transportability of both raw and manufactured goods, the revolution in communications and data processing, and the widespread dispersion of knowledge and technical skills throughout the global business community all have served to heighten competitiveness and weaken U.S. multinational preeminence in overseas markets.

INNOVATION

Innovation abroad here is defined as the development, manufacturing, and marketing of a new technology, product, or service for sale in a foreign market, *before* it is introduced in the U.S. market. Innovations may be either incremental or radical in nature. An early example of innovating for markets abroad is Pentaconta, a mechanical telephone switch developed by ITT in the late 1940s that had, by the early 1950s, become the standard for Western Europe.[1]

The role of innovation abroad in developing U.S. multinational strategy has received little attention in the literature. In an attempt to glean relevant evidence, the author conducted a survey of sixty U.S. multinationals, of which fifteen (see Table 1.1) were found to have repeatedly and successfully innovated abroad (see the Appendix for a detailed explanation of this survey and for supporting material). These innovations were by no means isolated; all fifteen multinationals introduced at least five innovations and some as many as 100. These fifteen innovators also were notable in having established R&D and manufacturing facilities abroad, a condition viewed as being absolutely necessary for innovating successfully in foreign markets. Further, these innovations were only rarely the radical technological breakthroughs often (and erroneously) associated with U.S. multinationals; rather, they tended to be more incremental in nature—that is, they involved the transfer, extension, or new application of existing technologies or products in markets abroad.

Although this approach lacks the glamour of radical breakthroughs, Nathan Rosenberg, for one, argues persuasively that such incremental improvements produce the greatest efficiency gains.[2] Examples include a battery separator made from polyvinylchloride; improvements in electronic fuel injection sys-

Table 1.1
15 U.S. Multinationals Innovating Abroad in Survey

Bendix Corporation (now Allied Corporation)

Corning Glass Works

Deere & Company

Dow Chemical Company

E.I. duPont de Nemours & Company

Firestone Tire & Rubber Company

Ford Motor Company

General Motors Corporation

GTE

Goodyear Tire & Rubber Company

W.R. Grace and Company

IBM

ITT

3M

TRW

Source: Survey

tems; and development of a resin for use in underwater offshore drilling rigs. All items underwent a period of R&D lasting from six months to as long as four years. Although the survey did not address the effectiveness of these innovations, the fact that all fifteen firms continued to innovate abroad strongly suggests that the strategy was perceived to be successful.

A BRIEF HISTORICAL SUMMARY:
POST–WORLD WAR II

The literature on the growth and development of the U.S. multinational shows that, in the three decades following World

War II—a period during which most other industrialized nations were in the process of reconstructing their war-damaged economies—U.S. multinationals experienced unprecedented growth and dominance in foreign markets. Put simply, the process worked as follows: A U.S. company first developed and introduced a new technology, product, or service for sale in the U.S. market, which at the time was vast, relatively homogeneous, well-known, and affluent. The domestic market for new products, both practical and leisure-oriented, seemed boundless, and U.S. companies responded with a tremendous outpouring of manufactured goods.

It followed naturally that, as particularly Western European economies became stronger, these U.S. companies then expanded into foreign markets. Accordingly, they exported domestically developed products to foreign consumers, and enjoyed great success. Gradually they discovered that it was more economically efficient to base certain business activities, particularly R&D and manufacturing, in the host countries themselves. And so, U.S. firms evolved into what we now call "multinationals," companies based at home but also doing business in many markets abroad.[3]

Two points regarding how these U.S. multinationals were structured are important. First, in the period immediately following World War II, those veterans who returned to enter managerial positions in U.S. multinationals brought with them intimate knowledge of the hierarchical military structure that had led the Allies to victory. Rather than retaking occupied territory, these managers now wished to establish beachheads in new markets abroad. As a result of their experiences in the war, they transferred knowledge of, and confidence in, the American military structure, with its highly formalized, compartmentalized approach to achieving goals, to the structuring of U.S. multinationals.

Related to this point is Alfred D. Chandler's assertion that such corporations as duPont and GM installed *managers* as corporate CEOs, rather than the entrepreneurs who had founded the firms.[4] Early in their growth (both pre– and post–World War II) these corporations developed control systems that were geared to long planning horizons, organized their basic structure around a system of divisions and departments that reported to centralized authorities, and assessed performance based upon managers' ability to allocate resources efficiently and to maintain or increase profits over the short term. All these approaches essentially duplicated the hierarchical structure of the U.S. military. And the approach indeed succeeded in achieving the U.S. multinationals' goal of penetrating markets abroad—but only until that point when vigorous competition from both other U.S. and non–U.S. multinationals and from national firms changed the rules of the game. The problem was that the rigid and hierarchical structures of U.S. multinationals under these new circumstances were in some ways ill-suited to respond to these new conditions and, as a rule-of-thumb, the more entrenched and rigid a hierarchical structure, the more difficult it is to change.

Planted in the background was another historical fact, one that eventually would play out to the advantage of the two major powers defeated by the Allies in World War II, Germany and Japan. The terms of unconditional surrender included stipulations that neither country could construct an offense-oriented military system, and war-potential industries were forbidden in Japan. The longer-term consequences of this decision could not possibly be foreseen amid the war-torn rubble of the time. Forced to abrogate any military growth, Germany and Japan were freed to devote their cultural and economic energies first to rebuilding their decimated countries and second, to devoting the full force of their national resources to business activities, both domestic and foreign. The scenario may have taken some two decades to play out, and not even the most gifted readers of tea leaves could have foretold the result. Although it is true that the United States post–World War II military research, development, and construction programs themselves led to a stream of innovations with non-military commercial applications, Germany and Japan incorporated into their economic and industrial reconstruction efforts the modernization of manufacturing, transportation, communications, and other industries to near state-of-the-art levels. This edge would, in the late 1960s and early 1970s, prove a formidable advantage when these two countries, and others in Western Europe, shifted focus from domestic to foreign business markets.

Coupled with this was another unforeseeable event: the OPEC oil embargo of 1973 and subsequent oil price shocks. The reverberations of OPEC's actions on the industrialized world are still being felt today, and in fundamental ways have altered the economies of once oil-dependent nations. In the United States, these included one moderately major recession and several modest ones. The position of the dollar fell, weakened relative to other currencies, and with it, balance-of-payments, export, and trade advantages that the U.S. for years had taken for granted. U.S. multinationals, their activities partly dependent upon stable foreign currency exchange rates and the affluence of consumers both domestic and foreign, were faced with declining market shares abroad and eroding assets, and many, by necessity, reacted by retrenching their positions. Once long-stable energy prices and supplies entered a period of often wild swings, which in turn affected other major factors of production; equilibrium was replaced by uncertainty. Although non–U.S. and national firms suffered as well, the Japanese yen and German mark both soon recovered relative to the U.S. dollar, thus giving further impetus for their challenge of U.S. multinationals in foreign markets.

These events, however, explain only a fraction of the influences facing U.S. multinationals in recent years. A review of the literature of international business and technology management illuminates several other crucial aspects, and perhaps none is more important than Raymond Vernon's development of the concept of the product life-cycle model.

AN ANALYSIS AND SUMMARY OF THE LITERATURE ON U.S. MULTINATIONALS

It was Raymond Vernon who in 1971 first looked at the growth of U.S. firms into multinationals and from his observations developed the "product life-cycle" model concept.

Vernon's model suggests that U.S. firms first entered international markets through the export of products initially developed for the U.S. market. As products become increasingly standardized through incremental refinements and improvements, supporting technologies, manufacturing characteristics, and even knowledge of demand and market characteristics became increasingly diffused to potential national competitors. Vernon suggests that when these national-firm competitors began to encroach upon U.S.–held markets, aided in part by the policies of their respective governments (such as advantageous tariffs, favorable tax policies, and R&D subsidies) and in part by gains in economies of scale, U.S. firms reacted by siting manufacturing facilities abroad. And as U.S.–developed products matured and as competitors began marketing their own versions of them, U.S. multinationals reacted by exporting still more innovations developed in the United States. This is the essence of Vernon's life-cycle model.

The literature on technology management, seen through Vernon's construct, expands upon this characterization of U.S. multinational behavior.[5] William Abernathy and James Utterback, for instance, demonstrate that as a product becomes standardized, its characteristics related to innovation also change. This change takes place in three basic stages.[6]

In the first stage, the product is introduced into a given market, and the firm concentrates efforts on modifying it to meet expected demand. Basic R&D, of course, is already complete.

In the second stage—the transitional stage—lengths of production runs increase, and prices become more competitive. At this point firms reap their greatest benefits both from R&D labs geared to further modifying the product and from improved efficiencies in the manufacturing process.

In the third and final stage, the product becomes highly standardized and production runs even longer. Activities focus almost exclusively on improving and extending manufacturing processes, and marketing strategies gain in prominence. R&D expenditures relative to total sales drop.

Following the schema of the life-cycle model concept, U.S. multinationals appear to undertake manufacturing abroad during the second (transitional) stage. At the time multinationals were establishing manufacturing facilities abroad, their products indeed were becoming standardized and production runs longer. However, the fact that many of these firms were also R&D intensive suggests that certain technologies were still undergoing *basic* changes, as were some manufacturing processes.

As products become increasingly standardized, manufacturing technologies begin to diffuse to competitors in both domestic and foreign markets.[7] Indeed, it was the diffusion to and adaptation of technologies by competitors in markets abroad that first led some U.S. firms to react by establishing manufacturing facilities overseas.[8] Absent this threat to market share, it is likely that U.S. multinationals would have continued to serve foreign markets through export of U.S. manufactured goods alone.

Another major point from the literature is that most firms innovate abroad as a defensive reaction, as innovations introduced by one firm threaten the market shares of competing firms. This happens in one of two ways. First, new products may simply capture market share at the expense of competitors. Second, the development of new processes may result in lowered manufacturing costs, thus allowing either price cuts and/or increased profits to the innovating firm. As both Rosenberg and F. M. Scherer point out, competitors usually respond to these types of threats by introducing competing technologies.[9]

Competition, Oligopoly, Imitation/Retaliation, and Cannibalization

Before examining revisions and extensions of Vernon's concept, it is helpful to broaden the context by summarizing the literature's understanding of how certain factors influence a U.S. multinational's response to competition, particularly in overseas markets. The major determinant of behavior is the fact that many U.S. corporations and almost all large U.S. multinationals are members of an oligopoly. This in turn impacts the nature of their response to competition, which may take one of two basic forms: imitation/retaliation, or cannibalization of existing products.

A traditional behavioral pattern for oligopoly members is to react to competition *imitatively*. Thus, when one U.S. multinational moves abroad, others in the same industry follow suit. Likewise, retaliatory actions by U.S. and non–U.S. multinationals in the same industry are not uncommon. For instance, a foreign-based corporation might open a subsidiary in the United States soon after a U.S. multinational opened a subsidiary on its competitor's home turf. Most corporations in an oligopoly act alike, so no one member will be substantively any better off than any others. If all enter the same foreign market simultaneously and fail, all suffer more or less equally. This imitative/retaliatory response underscores a basic characteristic of oligopoly members: their innate drive to maintain homeostatis, stability.

This characteristic applies as well to U.S. multinational attitudes to innovation. Innovation by one corporation has a potentially critical destabilizing effect on the industry as a whole. The introduction of new products or processes may change cost structures and renovate apportionment of market shares, sometimes dramatically. Since no corporation prefers uncertainty over predictability—stability is a vital ingredient in the success of long-range planning—and since the introduction of innovation shatters stability throughout the entire industry, oligopoly members as a rule would tend to avoid it.

This leads to the issue of cannibalizing existing product lines. Cannibalizing existing products effectively reduces the return on investment over what would accrue if sales of existing products were prolonged. Carliss Baldwin demonstrates disincentives to cannibalize, arguing that to maximize return on investment, a corporation should pace its rate of innovation such as to not cannibalize existing products. If the entire industry were developing new products at a rapid pace, cannibalization would follow close behind.[10] However, since most U.S. multinationals are members of an oligopoly, the *rate* of innovation is protracted such that each individual multinational attempts to maximize its return by, in effect, coordinating innovation strategies. But this balance is obviously upset when competitors, particularly non–U.S. multinationals and national firms, begin introducing or even simply *developing* new products and processes.

The salient point here is that the infusion into foreign markets of innovations developed by non–U.S. competitors puts pressures on oligopolistic U.S. multinationals to alter their current existing strategies. Once again, external pressures are forcing them to reassess the viability of past business practices, and it is not coincidental that closer examination of the problem finds the old bugbear of innovation once again lying underneath the carpet. Keeping these observations in mind, we now turn to an examination of how extensions and refinements of the product life-cycle concept can usefully address the current dilemma faced by U.S. multinationals.

The Product Life-Cycle Model Extended and Refined

In recent years, in response to the above-enumerated influences, several tenets underlying Vernon's product life-cycle concept have been subjected to an adaptive interpretation; indeed, the progenitor himself has recast several of his original premises.

The first centers on Vernon's understanding of the nature of technology transfer. Originally he hypothesized that, by focusing on U.S. firms and U.S. markets as the source of innovation, managers exhibit a myopic vision. The avoidance of certain uncertainties inherent in innovating for markets abroad led U.S. multinationals to site R&D facilities near corporate headquarters.

As U.S. multinationals expand their operations abroad, they do so by undertaking lower-cost and lower-risk activities first. Corporations, like most of earth's creatures, are cautious and conservative by nature. Thus, U.S. multinationals first entered foreign markets through exports, a low-cost, low-risk approach, then, encountering an initial spate of competition, they shored up their position by establishing sales and marketing offices abroad and, finally, by establishing manufacturing and R&D facilities abroad. Thus, the sequence of activities by U.S. multinationals moved incrementally from the least expensive and least risky to the more expensive and complex.

As we have seen, much research tends to support the validity of the product life-cycle model approach, both as it relates to the growth of U.S. multinationals and to the development and eventual transfer of new products from U.S. to foreign markets. Alternative hypotheses, however, may shed alternative light on this issue.

The contention is not that Vernon's concept fails to adequately depict the motivations underlying a U.S. multinational's response(s) to competition in foreign markets, but rather that recent, externally derived changes in those markets have altered the conditions under which Vernon originally developed the product life-cycle model. The above discussion of how the rise of competition in foreign markets might affect an oligopoly's member's view of innovation hints at the critical issue, and here it is made explicit: certain recent changes have had profound impact on what might *motivate* a U.S. multinational to innovate abroad. Two areas are discussed: first, briefly, vertical integration, and second, at greater length, intangible assets.

Vertical Integration. Vernon's product life-cycle concept omits any consideration of how vertical integration by a U.S. multinational might reduce certain critical transactional costs or potentially prohibitive uncertainties, the elimination of which might well affect a firm's motivations to innovate abroad. For example, a U.S. multinational whose primary activity is the manufacture of aluminum-based products, if perceiving potentially costly imperfections in bauxite production overseas, might choose both to eliminate certain direct and indirect transactional costs and to ensure quality, stability of supply, and price predictability of that bauxite by vertically integrating into direct ownership of mines and manufacturing facilities abroad. This influences the product life-cycle process in two ways: First, such vertical integration in effect results in the *post facto* creation of overseas subsidiaries. Second, the motivation for such action derives not from product life-cycle considerations but rather from the desire to reduce either transactional costs and/or supply/price uncertainties.

Intangible Assets. An even greater influence on a U.S. multinational's motivation to undertake innovation abroad, and one also unaccounted for by Vernon's life-cycle model, is what might be termed "intangible asset" concerns. Intangible assets are those assets that allow a multinational to maintain a competitive advantage in any given market over a sustained period of time. Examples include the deployment of technology monopolies, the strengths of a firm's R&D facilities, low advertising costs due to skilled marketing, the benefits of consumer loyalty to a brand name, and so forth. Although unmeasurable in dollar amounts, intangible assets bring the possessor-multinational advantages that cannot be dissipated by direct competition alone.

The point should not be taken lightly. As with vertical integration, the presence of intangible assets may help motivate a U.S. multinational to enter foreign markets, particularly when certain imperfections exist in those markets.

Intangible assets cannot be bought or sold like a physical commodity. For example, a U.S. multinational could hardly sell a technology to a competitor for a price that would equal the capitalized-value profit that that multinational would have received had it used the technology exclusively itself in that market. This is so because the foreign competitor would have doubts about the nuts-and-bolts effectiveness of the technology, as well as about the multinational's integrity as to how it represented the marketability of the technology.

If a multinational that expended millions or even hundreds of millions of dollars to develop a new technology or product were to sell the rights to it to a competitor, it would be prohibitive (and impossible to calculate economically) to include in the selling price expenditures associated with product R&D, organizational restructuring, marketing research, and so forth. Further, if the potential competitor-buyer could gain access to the technology through cost-free processes (such as routine technology transfer), it could benefit from the multinational seller's original and vast expenditures while paying nothing. For these reasons, the multinational seeks to house its technology within the confines of its organization. It takes competitors time and risk-related expenditures first to analyze and assess a new technology or product and then to retool its manufacturing and marketing facilities to produce it. Thus, by launching an innovation into the market ahead of competitors, the innovating multinational gains a first-move advantage.

Impacted information and opportunism costs represent one of the greatest disincentives for a multinational to license or sell its technology. The innovating firm values the information crucial to that technology at one price (see above), and a potential buyer has a disincentive for paying the market value that the innovating multinational might receive if it were to market that innovation abroad itself. Obviously, although a competitor may recognize the value of the technology, that value is diminished by the price it must pay for it. Thus, the potential buyer values the technology differently than does the innovating multinational, whose costs are already sunk. Further, the competitor lacks crucial information that the multinational has developed in the process of producing the innovation. And in negotiating a selling price, the competitor may disagree strongly with the multinational seller about the marketability, demand for, and worthiness of the innovation.

Licensing agreements present similar hazards, particularly when there is the threat of opportunism. For example, even if a multinational and a foreign supplier could negotiate a "perfect" contract at one given moment, over time an opportunity might arise for one or both parties to engage in exploitative behavior against the other, under terms of that contract. In the case of a multinational seller, it might discover that the buyer is not producing the technology according to specifications contracted for, or that the buyer is mismarketing the technology; this may detract from the royalty payments that the multinational would have received if it had licensed or sold the technology elsewhere, or if it had marketed it itself. This also might happen if the buyer lowered prices in order to compete with a similar but inferior product. Under these circumstances, the multinational could hardly find a new competitor-buyer without risking further damage to the market or increasing the number of competitors selling that technology.

The uncertainty that potential buyers face also looms as a factor that depresses the price (value) of the technology being sold. The potential buyer who operates in a foreign market may be unable to determine whether the product can be manufactured as efficiently in France, say, as it is in the United States. Or the buyer may be unable to compute the market demand for a product with sufficient confidence to warrant its purchase. Thus, a foreign firm whose managers are risk-averse are likely to undervalue the technology and would tend not to pay the market price that the multinational seller could obtain if it manufactured and sold the product abroad itself.

The foreign buyer thus faces two sources of uncertainty—in manufacturing costs and in marketability—and both lead the buyer to substantially discount the U.S. multinational's valuation of the technology. Thus, the multinational seller faces two alternatives: losing the opportunity of selling, or selling but at the risk of incurring the potential losses of not obtaining a return on its sunk investments and at the risk of seeing the technology diffuse prematurely.

The foregoing illustrates the fundamental difference between the product life-cycle approach and the transaction costs/intangible assets approach to analyzing multinational innovation abroad. The life-cycle approach emphasizes patterns; the transaction costs/intangible assets approach emphasizes *motivations*.

The life-cycle approach was developed during the post–World War II, pre–1973 embargo period, a period that saw continual expansion by U.S. multinationals into markets abroad. But conditions have changed since then. The U.S. market no longer necessarily offers the most affluent customers or highest-cost labor force, nor does it necessarily draw upon the most highly skilled scientists and technicians. In a number of major industries, Japanese and Western European companies have gained decisive leads over the United States. Further, the phenomenal developments in electronic communications over the past decade have facilitated the process of technology transfer and at the same time have eroded some basic advantages of innovating first in the home market. Now managers in U.S. multinationals can, with relative ease, analyze and assess the characteristics of markets in South America or India almost as accurately (or poorly) as they can those in the United States. Further, as U.S. multinationals have increasingly established manufacturing and R&D facilities in countries abroad, the presence of these subsidiary firms has further facilitated the development of innovations abroad.

All these factors weighed together act to expose the limitations of the product life-cycle approach in explaining recent U.S. multinational behavior toward innovating abroad. Vernon's approach emphasizes patterns, patterns based upon defensive behavior, but all multinationals do not innovate abroad for defensive reasons alone, and indeed a trend seems to be developing wherein some are choosing a more proactive strategy. It is not that Vernon sheds no light, for many of his constructs still apply, particularly concerning the relationship of technology monopoly to the three basic stages of subsidiary growth; it is more that conditions have changed such that Vernon no longer holds absolute sway. The old patterns have been broken, and in their place another interpretation is taking hold. This approach, as exemplified by the vertical integration/intangible assets discussion, focuses more upon *motivation* as being the primary key underlying decisions by U.S. multinationals to innovate abroad as a conscious proactive strategy.

A NEW APPROACH

This book addresses three fundamental questions in context of the foregoing discussion:

1. What circumstances and conditions motivate U.S. multinationals to innovate abroad?
2. What characteristics distinguish U.S. multinationals that successfully innovate abroad from those that do not?
3. How might U.S. multinationals integrate innovation abroad into their overall strategies?

Part I addresses the first two questions; Part II, the third.

Accordingly, Chapter 2 examines how three general factors impact the viability of innovating abroad. Technology monopoly is addressed in this new context, followed by a discussion of the sources of competition in foreign markets. The chapter concludes with an assessment of the firm's overall market orientation (local versus world). The core contention here is that U.S. multinationals innovate abroad primarily when they perceive competitive threat to their market positions abroad.

Chapter 3, drawing in part upon a survey of sixty multinationals conducted by the author, then compares innovating and noninnovating companies in terms of the influences of R&D intensity, commitment to international growth objectives, and firm size. The discussion then turns to two other equally important issues: the influence of actual experience in lowering uncertainty in four areas (market, political, technical, and labor), and the impact of how the corporate parent organizes for international sales (international division, product line or geographical area).

Chapter 4 shifts focus to the central concern of the book, which contends that the time is ripe for U.S. multinationals to move from a defensive to a more proactive strategy toward innovating in markets abroad. The chapter examines the three basic classes of subsidiaries (technology monopoly, product, and service) in the context of how they use internal and external resources in responding to the survival-threatening crises to which any innovation-oriented endeavor is subject. These three classes are then associated with three fundamental approaches to proactively innovating (team, dual [technology/marketing], and financial), and each is assessed in terms of their determining influences and objectives, including technology monopoly, market/demand, risk, and related issues. This chapter forms the basis from which more direct influences on innovating are assessed. Taken together, these three chapters outline those conditions that are absolutely necessary for a U.S. multinational to successfully innovate in markets abroad, and also outline the basis for the defensive reaction approach, the approach from which a new, proactive strategy must in part derive.

Part II then addresses question three: What changes are necessary for a defensively-oriented U.S. multinational to shift to a proactive strategy?

Accordingly, Chapter 5 examines how control systems can be structured and managed to serve nontraditional (innovation-oriented) objectives in such ways that they draw and apply valuable experience from the crises and uncertainties endemic to innovating firms. This chapter draws upon a survey of fifty small, U.S.-based, start-up entrepreneurial firms and applies results of the survey to define how control systems can be designed for subsidiaries innovating abroad. Four basic components of these control systems—planning, budgeting, performance measures, and incentive systems—are examined.

As crucial as flexible, adaptive control systems are to surviving crises and lessening uncertainties, they are at heart only tools to be used in the hands of managers, the subject of Chapters 6 and 7. In the final analysis, managers are the penultimate determinant of whether an innovating subsidiary will rise or fall, and so the managerial qualities needed to serve a proactive strategy are enumerated. Major focus is given to the "organizational entrepreneur," the individual who must work within an existing corporate structure to bring an innovation to the point of commercial fruition.

NOTES

1. ITT, "Telecommunications and Economics," pp. 1–2.

2. Nathan Rosenberg, "The Direction of Technological Change: Inducement Mechanisms and Focusing Devices," in *Economic Development and Cultural Change,* no. 1, pt. 1 (October 1969).

3. See, for example, Raymond Vernon, *Sovereignty at Bay: The Multinational Spread of U.S. Enterprises* (New York: Basic Books, 1971), pp. 3–25, 60–112; and John H. Dunning, "Technology Transfer," in Charles P. Kindleberger (ed.), *The International Corporation* (Cambridge, Mass.: MIT Press, 1970), pp. 141–76.

4. Alfred D. Chandler, Jr., *Strategy and Structure: Chapters in the History of the American Industrial Enterprise* (Cambridge, Mass.: MIT Press, 1962).

5. Various authors discuss the effects of technological differences between the United States and other countries. See J. Servan-Schreiber, *The American Challenge* (London: Hamish Hamilton, 1968); S. Hirsch, *Location of Industry and International Competitiveness* (Oxford, England: Clarendon Press, 1967); and F. M. Adler and G. C. Hufbauer, *Overseas Manufacturing Investment: The Balance of Payments,* (Washington, D.C.: U.S. Department of Commerce, 1968). For further discussion of the product life-cycle model, see Raymond Vernon, "International Investment and International Trade in the Product Cycle," *in Quarterly Journal of Economics, 80* (1966), pp. 190–207, and Louis T. Wells, Jr., ed., *The Product Life Cycle and International*

Trade (Boston: Harvard University Graduate School of Business Administration, Division of Research, 1972).

6. William J. Abernathy and James M. Utterback, "Innovation and the Evolving Structure of the Firm," Harvard University Graduate School of Business Paper no. 75–18 (Boston, June 1975).

7. See, for example, Edwin Mansfield, *Industrial Research and Technological Innovation: An Econometric Analysis* (New York: W. W. Norton & Company, 1968), pp. 133–94.

8. Robert B. Stobaugh, Jr., et al., *Nine Investments Abroad and Their Impact at Home* (Boston: Harvard University Graduate School of Business Administration, Division of Research, 1976).

9. F. M. Scherer, *Industrial Market Structure and Economic Performance* (Chicago: Rand McNally College Publishing Co., 1970), pp. 366–78; also Rosenberg, "The Direction of Technological Change."

10. Carliss Baldwin, "Time Inconsistency in Capital Budgeting," Harvard University Graduate School of Business Paper no. 89–002 (June 1988).

2

Technology Monopoly, Competition Sources, and Market Orientation

Just as the decision by U.S. multinationals to site both manufacturing and R&D facilities abroad was a defensive reaction to competitive threat, so too historically has been their decision to *innovate* in foreign markets. Particularly during the last decade, they have increasingly encountered serious competition in nearly every major foreign market.[1] BASF manufactures an array of photographic films that directly compete with those of Kodak; Bosch manufactures fuel injection systems that compete with those of Bendix; SONY and Philips manufacture electrical appliances that compete with those of RCA and General Electric. The core contention of this chapter is that U.S. multinationals will not be motivated to innovate abroad unless they perceive a critical vulnerability or threat to their market positions abroad. And of all motivations to innovate, the threat (either actual or potential) of competition is the most fundamental and persuasive. Absent competition and some meaningful stake in preserving market share abroad, most multinationals historically demonstrate little motivation to become entrepreneurial by innovating abroad.[2]

This chapter turns to how three basic factors have historically impacted a U.S. multinational's decision and likelihood of success in innovating abroad: the status of technology monopolies, the sources of competition, and the firm's market orientation (local versus world). Examination of each factor yields valuable insight upon which other multinationals can draw when considering whether and how they should venture down the same path.

THE DECLINE OF TECHNOLOGY MONOPOLIES

Although a thing of beauty, a technology monopoly cannot, unlike a diamond, last forever. As a product is sold in open markets, potential competitors gradually will gain knowledge of the proprietary technologies involved until, in time, most of the original advantages underlying the technology monopolies are lost. This problem has taken on increasing importance for U.S. multinationals in recent years as competitors, particularly those innovating specifically for foreign markets, have superseded U.S. multinational technology monopolies with those of their own. The Japanese marketing of smaller automobiles in the United States following the 1973 OPEC embargo is one such example.

Some technology monopolies last longer than others.[3] In large part this is dependent upon the degree of specialization of the product, its breadth of application, and the ambition and ability of other resource-capable competitors to enter the market.

For example, RCA's preeminence in the manufacture of satellite telecommunications equipment has gone largely unchallenged for decades. This is attributable to the enormous capital outlay involved in performing both the necessary direct and indirect R&D, the highly specialized nature of the technology, the nondiffuse, narrow market, and the dearth of potential competitors having the financial, technological, and organizational resources crucial to such an undertaking.

On the other hand, both Sylvania and Philips almost simultaneously introduced incandescent light bulbs into Western European markets. In this instance, the two multinationals were motivated to defend against the other's capture of a potentially highly lucrative market, and both possessed the resources and had access to the (relatively unsophisticated) technologies necessary to develop the product.

With these examples in mind, what then are the forces that

define and determine the strength, value, and duration of a technology monopoly, and how do they affect a U.S. multinational's decision to innovate for markets abroad?

First, as stated in the earlier discussion of the product life-cycle model, the strength of a technology monopoly relates directly to the maturity of that technology (or product). In its earliest stages, the strength of a technology monopoly is almost absolute, and there are no or few competitors. During this period, proprietary processes and product R&D are held very close to the chest. However, over time the innovation becomes increasingly standardized and, as the preeminent multinational gains in experience, a number of manufacturing and marketing uncertainties are overcome. The lessening of uncertainty and increasing familiarity with the technology and market increase the motivation for potential competitors to undertake imitative production of that product. As more and more competitors venture into the fray, manufacturing and marketing uncertainties are further reduced.[4] The technology thus becomes increasingly diffused and over time its monopoly advantages wither away; at this point, the technology can be said to have become "mature."

Of course, the originating multinational still has the opportunity to protect its market share through incremental improvements to the product, but the gains from such a strategy usually become proportionately lower as diffusion broadens; the broader the diffusion, the more likely competitive firms are to encroach upon market share. In some cases this might be an argument for a multinational to consider focusing attention on *new* innovations, particularly if it has lost its initial advantages so completely that the original product is no longer profitable.

The impact of uncertainty on potential competitors is another major influence.[5] When a new technology is successfully introduced into a given market, competitors considering an imitative response find themselves facing daunting R&D, market, manufacturing, technical, and financial uncertainties. Lacking any hands-on experience with the costs of manufacturing that new technology, having no access to the proprietary technologies, and possessing none of the R&D and technology monopoly advantages residing with the originating multinational, most potential competitors will opt to wait until technology diffusion is well underway before entering the market. However, there are potential lost opportunity costs associated with such behavior; because an innovative technology that gains wide market acceptance tends to establish a new, industry-wide standard, existing competitors in that industry sooner or later will be forced to adapt to this new standard. Thus, there are potentially crippling costs associated with pursuing either strategy—quickly, imitatively innovating or biding one's time. The problem is even worse for start-up competitors, who are trebly handicapped by resource constraints, a variety of uncertainties, and the absence of direct experience operating in the market. They thus would be least likely to enter the fray.

Thus, the successful introduction of an innovation based on a technology monopoly creates significant barriers to entry to *all* potential competitors. This further compounds the advantages of technology monopoly enjoyed by the originating multinational, and moreover acts to lengthen the lifetime of that monopoly.[6] For these reasons, pursuing a technology monopoly strategy may be a highly attractive option for some U.S. multinationals in some markets abroad.

As shown in Chapter 1, the foreign market positions of U.S. multinationals have shifted significantly. In the two decades following World War II, U.S. multinationals enjoyed strong technological advantages in foreign markets, which they buttressed by siting manufacturing and, in some cases, R&D facilities in those markets. Although competitors soon began imitating and marketing U.S.- developed products, they lacked the underlying expertise and technological and economic strengths of U.S. firms, so high-threat, toe-to-toe competition initially was only modest and fragmented.[7]

By 1980, however, U.S. multinationals no longer possessed such a preeminence of technological monopolies in foreign markets. As stated earlier, a number of factors combined to undermine the U.S. position, including the rising economic strengths of Japan, West Germany, and other industrialized nations, the negative impacts of OPEC-driven oil price hikes, the adherence of U.S. multinationals to time-tested but suddenly less responsive strategies, and so forth. Equally important was the gradually accumulating experience of competing firms, whose (mostly imitative) responses to U.S. multinationals, however modest, brought them four-square into the new age of high-tech, globally-directed business. Put simply, they gradually acquired the base from which later to launch full-scale assaults in certain markets.

Interviews by the author with fifty-seven out of sixty U.S. multinational managers underscored their awareness of intensified and technically adroit competition, beginning around 1970. Of the three firms that did not perceive significant threat to their product lines overseas (Polaroid, RCA, and Combustion Engineering), their managers reported that they perceived no *need* to innovate abroad. Instead, all three firms reported sustaining growth abroad exclusively through technology transfers from parent to subsidiary abroad, a strategy that succeeded essentially because foreign technological expertise in these product lines lagged far behind their own. Thus, the *absence* of competition may be perceived as a *disincentive* to innovate: in essence, a "why-rock-the-boat" scenario. As a manager from one of these firms states:

Let me put it like this: So long as our company maintains its product position and there are no genuine heavyweight competitors, and so long as demand continues to grow, *we* define the state-of-the-art technology. When competitors enter into the market with a similar technology, then we begin to transfer technology from our U.S. base into those foreign markets at a faster rate. The competition is developing similar products faster than before, but our demand position is still stable. My point is that so long as we can produce innovations in the United States and successfully transfer them to growing markets abroad, we would not see much rationale to innovate in foreign countries. However, if competitors were to get a technological leg up over us, so to speak, we might change our mind. But not until then.[8]

Managers of the other fifty-seven firms all confirmed in interviews that they undertook innovation abroad in direct reaction to threats of encroachment by competitors in foreign markets. Indeed, the threat of competition historically has con-

stituted a necessary and even absolute precondition to innovating abroad.

A number of these managers pointed out that these threats
fall into two classes: actual and potential. Actual threats arise
from the successful introduction of innovations by competitors.
Potential threats are more indirect or "hidden"; they include
such factors as the size and emphasis of a competitor's R&D
budget; the number, type, and sophistication of technologists,
engineers, and scientists; the technical skill-level of the host-
country labor force; government policies (taxes, licensing, subsidies for R&D or manufacturing) in support of national firms;
and so forth. Managers from all fifty-seven multinationals
unanimously cited the presence of either one or both forms of
threat as motivating them to innovate abroad.

THE SOURCES OF COMPETITION

The second major influence on whether and how a U.S. multinational innovates abroad focuses upon the sources of potential competition in foreign markets. There are three: other U.S.
multinationals, non–U.S. multinationals, and national (or local) firms in host countries.[9] Which of these competitors a multinational encounters will influence the markets for which it
innovates abroad.

Chapter 3 will explore how R&D intensity correlates with a
multinational's tendency to innovate abroad; this chapter examines how R&D intensity relates to the three sources of competition a U.S. multinational innovating abroad might expect
to encounter. There are three levels: highly R&D-intensive (3
percent or more of total sales allocated to R&D); moderately
R&D-intensive (1 to 3 percent); and low R&D-intensive (less
than 1 percent).

This last group tends to have the least degree of technical
orientation (see Chapter 3) and only poorly understands the
innovation process, either in domestic or foreign markets.
Hence, the group is unlikely to innovate abroad and need not
concern us here.

The sources of competition faced by moderately R&D-inten-
sive multinationals are equally as clear. Since their technol-

Table 2.1

Sources of Competition for Innovating U.S. Multinationals by R&D Intensity

Level of R&D Intensity	Number of Firms that Perceive Competition From:			
	Other U.S. Multinationals	Non-U.S. Multinationals	National Firms	Number of Firms in Sample
Moderate	10	8	10	10
High	5	5	2	5

Source: Survey

ogies are more likely to have already diffused to competitors, they are likely to encounter competition from all three sources (again, see Chapter 3 for further discussion).

Table 2.1 presents the sources of competition, as perceived by managers in the fifteen U.S. multinationals identified in the author's survey as being innovators abroad. Results support the contention that moderately R&D-intensive firms experience competition from all three sources (all ten perceived threats from both national and U.S.–based firms; and eight additionally also perceived it from non–U.S. multinationals.

The sources of competition faced by highly R&D-intensive multinationals are more varied and complex. One hypothesis is that because they enjoy relatively secure technology monopolies, their technologies have diffused only to other multinationals having the resources capable of competing. National firms that lack the necessary resources are priced out of the picture. In the event that, in that industry/market segment, other U.S., non–U.S. multinationals, and/or national firms *do* have the capability and inclination to develop competing technologies, then all three will be potential competitors.

All five highly R&D-intensive firms perceived competition from both U.S. and non–U.S. multinationals; but only two perceived it also from national firms. As postulated above, this suggests that some U.S. multinationals may still exercise technological or other advantages over national firms, but not over other U.S. and non–U.S. multinationals. With this background in mind, we now examine each of the three sources of competition in turn.

Competition from Other U.S. Multinationals

The introduction or transfer of an innovation abroad by one U.S. multinational may provoke an imitative response from other U.S. multinationals operating in the same market. This is particularly true when firms are members of the same oligopoly, and are competing with similar products for shares of the same market. F. T. Knickerbocker has documented such reactive behavior, showing that the appearance of competitive threats in a given geographical market provokes imitative responses by firms in the same oligopoly, including establishing subsidiaries in that market nearly simultaneously.[10]

Member firms of some oligopolies offer very similar products, and compete for the same market share on relatively equal footing.[11] In such instances, an innovation introduced by one firm provokes an imitative response by the other, as fast and effectively as possible. For example, UniRoyal introduces a high-performance auto tire for European sports car enthusiasts and Goodyear, if sufficiently threatened, follows suit. Of course, oligopoly members competing in distinctly different markets—no matter how similar their products—only rarely will be motivated to engage in such imitative behavior; Deere, which produces tires for smaller tractors, has little motivation to respond to Caterpiller's introduction of tires for larger tractors in the same market.

Table 2.2 compares innovators and noninnovators in six U.S. industries, three of which (automotive, machinery, and rubber) show evidence of imitative responses through substitutable products. Thus, Ford and GM both originated their "world market cars" in West Germany; Deere and New Holland both produced their small tractor lines in Western Europe; and Firestone, Goodyear, and UniRoyal all developed radial tires in Western Europe.

Table 2.2
Number of Innovators and Noninnovators in Selected
Oligopolies, U.S.–based Multinationals

Industries With Direct Competition	Industries Without Direct Competition	Innovators	Noninnovators
Automotive		2	0
Machinery		2	0
Rubber		3	0
	Chemicals	2	2
	Computer	1	1
	Glass	1	1
Total		11	4

Note: This table compares industries having two or more firms, of which at least one innovated abroad. Although 15 multinationals in the survey innovated abroad, only 11 were in industries with 2 or more firms.

Source: Survey

In the other three industries (computers, glass, and chemicals), member firms developed their products for different market segments. For example, IBM developed a computer geared for the Japanese banking industry, a market segment Honeywell did not address. Corning introduced a new process for manufacturing sunglasses in France; Owens-Illinois did not. Finally, the chemical industry best epitomizes the nonimitative response of firms that offer different products (two firms innovated abroad; two did not). Dow introduced a new inorganic substance to be used in carpeting; duPont introduced an organic agricultural compound. The two firms that did not innovate abroad concentrated efforts on product lines geared to different market segments.

The correlations between innovations abroad by U.S. multinationals and competition from other U.S. multinationals in those markets are complex; some competing U.S. firms tend to imitate another U.S. multinational's innovations; others do not. The rule of thumb seems to be that the decision to innovate/imitate is based upon the perception of threat to market share; where it exists, imitation is much more likely than when it is not.

Competition from Non–U.S. Multinationals

What of competition from non–U.S. multinationals? Managers from the fifteen innovating U.S. multinationals report two sources of threat—actual and potential—either of which will provoke a competitive response from them[12]

Managers cited a number of examples of actual threat, where innovations by non–U.S. multinationals had captured a portion of their foreign and, in several instances, U.S. market shares. Both Ford and GM cited Volkswagen, BMW, Fiat, and various Japanese automotive companies, whose fuel-efficient cars were capturing significant market shares in both foreign and U.S. markets. UniRoyal and Goodyear cited Michelin's tires, and Bendix cited Bosch's electronic fuel injection system as threats to their market shares in Western Europe. W. R. Grace & Company developed a PVC battery separator in response to one introduced by BASF in West Germany.

A manager from Firestone Tire and Rubber Company expands upon the motivations for innovating defensively beyond considerations of profit and market shares as follows:

We have long been involved in developing tires both for new vehicles and as competitive replacements for existing vehicles. The competitive motivation to develop high-speed–rated radials derives from the fact that other tire companies, such as Michelin, Pirelli, and Continental, all are seeking to establish ongoing relationships with such prestigious European automakers as Porsche, Audi, Alfa Romeo, Mercedes, Volvo, and so on. From our point of view, the failure to meet this challenge not only would signal a potential loss of prestige and profit, but would signal to competitors and auto manufacturers alike that we were unwilling or unable to keep pace with the technology involved. And indeed, as our efforts succeeded, both our reputation and related profits have been bolstered.[13]

The example is salient not only as another instance of a U.S. multinational responding to competition from non–U.S. multinationals (and from national firms as well), but also as demonstrating that motivation may derive from a wish to protect intangible assets kinds of concerns (in this instance, prestige and maintenance of healthy, ongoing relationships with European automobile manufacturers).

These examples all suggest that innovations by non–U.S. multinationals indeed are making inroads into the foreign market shares of U.S. multinationals. As one U.S. executive put it:

In terms of guarding our foreign market shares, it used to be that we only had to keep an eye out on other U.S. firms, but all that has changed. Now it seems that in nearly every market where we operate, both at home and abroad, one or more of the big foreign firms is also there. Many of them are European firms that consider developing a new product for the European market the same as we consider developing new products for the U.S. market. So the world has changed. Now, in most foreign markets, we have to keep an eye out for what the foreign multinationals and even the locals are doing as well.[14]

What of potential threats? Here U.S. managers' concerns seem to lie predominantly with determining whether, if they did not act and non–U.S. multinationals did, the cost of lost opportunity would be high. The Firestone example above pertains here, and another U.S. multinational executive underscores this point by stating:

Our company *never* assumes that, say, a Western European or Japanese multinational cannot or will not address any need that we can. In fact, we are very aware of the fact that some foreign companies are now the leaders in certain technologies. We therefore assume that if a need exists, foreign competitors have at least the same capability to develop products to meet that need as we do.[15]

Thus, it is clear that the presence of either actual or potential threats to market share abroad by non–U.S. multinationals will tend to provoke a defensive, imitative response from U.S. multinationals doing business in those markets.

Competition from National Firms

Many national firms become capable of challenging U.S. multinationals only with the support of their governments, whether direct or indirect (through licensing restrictions on U.S. multinational activities in the host country, subsidies favorable to national firms, advantageous tax laws, and so forth).[16] This happens particularly in those industries deemed essential to national security, economic growth, or national prestige; examples include the aerospace, nuclear power, steel, and computer industries.

In some cases, this government support succeeds in raising national firms to levels comparable with those of U.S. multinationals. In West Germany, Kraftwerkunion depends upon government-sponsored R&D to build nuclear power plants that produce electricity for sale in both domestic and foreign markets, while Westinghouse, once the undisputed leader in the same markets, is struggling to earn a profit from its light-water reactors.[17]

Government support does not necessarily ensure success however. For example, several government-supported consortia in the United Kingdom failed in the past two decades to establish a viable nuclear power industry.[18] This may help explain why highly R&D-intensive U.S. multinationals perceive government-subsidized national firms, on the whole, as less threatening than do moderately R&D-intensive multinationals.

The manager of a U.S. computer company states it thus:

Sure, we sit up and take notice when foreign governments announce their intentions to support one industry or another. We watch very carefully; we have to. However, just because this or that government comes out and says, "Hey, we want to back this industry," we've learned not to act too precipitously. On a couple of occasions, we got burned. One minister said that his government would do thus and thus and then, by the time we had geared up to compete, the government had changed hands, and with it the priorities for industrial development. Now we've learned to wait long enough to be sure what will happen. Sometimes nothing does.[19]

Thus, it appears that innovative U.S. multinationals perceive a threat only from national firms that possess the necessary resources to compete, which frequently they do only with governmental support: Yet even then, they may fail as competitors. For this reason national firms are regarded, on the whole, as posing the least competitive threat to U.S. multinational market shares abroad.

MARKETS FOR INNOVATION ABROAD

There are two basic markets for innovations: local and worldwide. Innovations for local markets are defined as those sold only in the market where originally introduced (although, if demand warrants, they eventually may be transferred elsewhere). Innovations for world markets are those that find immediate demand in one or more markets in addition to the local, originating market.

Table 2.3 indicates that most innovations abroad by U.S. multinationals are developed for local rather than world markets. Of thirty-six innovations by the fifteen innovating U.S. multinationals, twenty-two were for local markets (61 percent), while only fourteen were for world markets (39 percent). There are two explanations for this. First, there are a multitude of local markets for a multitude of different innovations, but only one world market for one type of innovation. Further, an innovation by one U.S. multinational might stimulate other, competing innovations from other U.S. multinationals. Second, the United States offers U.S. multinationals a highly attractive market from which to launch innovations into the world market. In the United States, there is readily available a vast pool of technically skilled personnel and the advantages of a centralized R&D facility situated near, and responsive to, corporate headquarters; in addition, the United States offers a large and affluent population into which first to introduce an innovation.

Table 2.3
Relation between R&D Intensity and Types of Markets for 36
Foreign Innovations

Level of R&D Intensity	Number of Foreign Innovations		
	For Local Markets	For World Markets	Total Innovations
Moderate	20	6	26
High	2	8	10
Totals	22	14	36

Note: Noninnovating firms from the survey are not included.
Source: Survey

Two general rules govern the relationship between market orientation and sources of competition for moderately and highly R&D-intensive U.S. multinationals.

First, because moderately R&D-intensive U.S. multinationals tend to encounter competition from national firms more so than highly R&D-intensive multinationals, it follows that the former are more likely to innovate for markets (although they may innovate for world markets as well). These multinationals tend to erect barriers to entry by national firms that are other than technological. Some, such as automotive firms, use the need for large-scale capital investment or high economies-of-scale in manufacturing processes to bar national firms; others may rely on advertising skills, brand-name loyalty, or other such intangible assets.

Second, highly R&D-intensive U.S. multinationals innovate abroad primarily for world markets. Because they perceive little significant competition from national firms, they are more likely to expend R&D costs for one single product and to gear it for sale in *many* regional markets, rather than to develop several products for many markets.

Table 2.3 supports these two general rules. Of the twenty-six innovations by moderately R&D-intensive U.S. multinationals, twenty were for local markets (77 percent), while of the ten innovations abroad by highly R&D-intensive multinationals, only two were for local markets (20 percent).

NOTES

1. The sources of competition in foreign markets were identified from author's interviews with managers of various U.S. multinationals. For supporting statistical evidence on the subject, see Robert B. Stobaugh, Jr., "Competition Encountered by U.S. Companies That Manufacture Abroad," in *Journal of International Business Studies,* Spring/Summer 1972, pp. 33–43.

2. Much evidence for U.S. multinationals' defensive behavior can be found in product life-cycle model and related research. For instance, see Raymond Vernon, "International Investment and International Trade in the Product Cycle," in *Quarterly Journal of Economics* 80 (1966) , pp. 190–207; Raymond Vernon, *Sovereignty at Bay: The Multinational Spread of U.S. Enterprises* (New York: Basic Books, 1971), pp. 3–25, 60–112; Louis T. Wells, Jr., ed., *The Product Life Cycle and International Trade* (Boston: Harvard University Graduate School of Business Administration, Division of Research, 1975); and Robert H. Hayes and William J. Abernathy, " Managing Our Way to Economic Decline," in *Harvard Business Review,* July/August 1980, pp. 67–77.

3. Raymond Vernon and W. H. Davidson, "Foreign Production of Technology-Intensive Products by U.S.–based Multinational Enterprises" (Boston: Harvard University Graduate School of Business Paper no. 79–5, 1979), pp. 1–148; Raymond Vernon, *Storm over the Multinationals: The Real Issues* (Cambridge, Mass.: Harvard University Press, 1977), pp. 39–58; and National Science Foundation, *Science Indicators, 1976, Report of the National Science Board 1977* (Washington, D.C.: U.S. Government Printing Office Stock no. 038–000–00341–1, 1977), pp. 1–41.

4. F. M. Scherer, *Industrial Market Structure and Economic Performance* (Chicago: Rand McNally College Publishing Co., 1970), pp. 366–78; Christopher Freeman, *The Economics of Industrial Innovation* (Baltimore: Penguin Books, 1974), pp. 253–82; D. C. Mueller and J. E. Tilton, "Research and Development Costs as a Barrier to Entry," in *Canadian Journal of Economics* 2, no. 4 (November 1970), pp. 570–79; Robert B. Stobaugh, Jr., "The Neotechnology Account of International Trade: The Case of Petrochemicals," in Wells, *The Product Life Cycle and International Trade,* pp. 83–110; and Raymond Ver-

non, "Gone Are the Cashcows of Yesteryear," in *Harvard Business Review,* November/December 1980, pp. 150–55.

5. William J. Abernathy and James M. Utterback, "Innovation and the Evolving Structure of the Firm," Harvard University Graduate School of Business Paper no. 75–18 (Boston, June 1975), pp. 1–31; and Freeman, *The Economics of Industrial Innovation,* pp. 74–107.

6. For further discussion, see William H. Gruber, Dileep Mehta, and Raymond Vernon, "The R&D Factor in International Trade and International Investment in U.S. Industries," in Wells, *The Product Life Cycle and International Trade,* pp. 111–39; Vernon, *Sovereignty at Bay,* pp. 77–89; Vernon, *Storm over the Multinationals,* pp. 39–58; Scherer, *Industrial Market Structure,* pp. 346–78; Edwin Mansfield, *Industrial Research and Technological Innovation: An Econometric Analysis* (New York: W. W. Norton Co., 1968); and Raymond Vernon, "Organization as a Scale Factor in the Growth of Firms," in J. W. Markham and G. F. Papanek (eds.), *Industrial Organization and Economic Development* (Boston: Houghton-Mifflin Co., 1970).

7. Vernon, *Sovereignty at Bay,* pp. 3–25, 60–112.

8. Author's interview of manager of a U.S. multinational, proprietary.

9. Much of this discussion draws upon Raymond Vernon's research. For a summary, see Vernon, *Storm over the Multinationals,* pp. 39–101.

10. See F. T. Knickerbocker, "Oligopolistic Reaction and Multinational Enterprises" (D.B.A. diss., Harvard University Graduate School of Business, 1974).

11. Peter J. Buckley and Mark Casson, "The Optimal Timing of a Foreign Direct Investment" (Reading, Pa.: University of Reading, Department of Economics, Working Paper no. 48, February 1980), pp. 1–20; Freeman, *The Economics of Industrial Innovation,* pp. 253–82; Michael E. Porter, "The Structure Within Industries and Companies' Performance," in *Review of Economics and Statistics* 10, May 19, 1970, pp. 214–27; Scherer, *Industrial Market Structure,* pp. 346–78; and Vernon, *Storm over the Multinationals,* pp. 59–101.

12. For a summary of the potential for foreign-based multinationals, see Stephen Hymer and Robert Rowthorn, "Multinational Corporations and International Oligopoly: The Non-American Challenge," in Charles P. Kindleberger (ed.), *The International Corporation* (Cambridge, Mass.: MIT Press, 1970); Stobaugh, "Competition Encountered by U.S. Companies"; and Vernon, *Storm over the Multinationals,* pp. 59–101. One might expect that U.S. multinationals are

in some way responding to territorial/market threats from non–U.S.-based multinationals; see E. M. Graham, "Oligopolistic Imitation and European Direct Investment in the United States" (D.B.A. diss., Harvard University Graduate School of Business, Boston, 1974).

13. Author's interview with a manager at Firestone Tire and Rubber Company, proprietary.

14. Author's interview with a manager of a U.S. multinational, proprietary.

15. Author's interview with a manager of a U.S. multinational, proprietary.

16. Vernon, *Storm over the Multinationals,* pp. 49–51, 103–38; H. R. Nau, *National Politics and International Technology* (Baltimore: Johns Hopkins University Press, 1974); and Kenneth N. Waltz, "The Myth of National Interdependence," in Charles P. Kindleberger, ed., *The International Corporation* (Cambridge, Mass.: MIT Press, 1970), pp. 205–23.

17. I. C. Bupp and J. C. Derian, *Light Water Reactors* (New York: Basic Books, 1978).

18. Vernon, *Storm over the Multinationals,* p. 51; and Bupp and Derian, *Light Water Reactors,* pp. 50–125.

19. Author's interview with a manager of a U.S. multinational, proprietary.

Strategic Factors

Chapter 2 assessed how technology monopolies, sources of competition, and market orientation all historically have impacted the decision by U.S. multinationals to innovate abroad. Attention now shifts from those general issues to assess how five specific factors influence the decision to innovate in foreign markets, yielding a general framework—or, more humbly, a "checklist"—with which U.S. multinationals can determine where their strengths and weaknesses lie. Drawing upon the author's survey of sixty multinationals, the discussion first focuses upon R&D intensity (measured in terms of foreign versus domestic R&D expenditures), prior commitment to growth abroad (measured in terms of total versus foreign sales), and size (measured in relative assets, circa 1979); and then turns to the effects of actual experience operating abroad (particularly as regards reducing critical uncertainties) and of various forms of organizational structures. As in Chapter 2, the discussion illuminates a set of factors deemed necessary (or, more accurately, "sufficient") for U.S. multinationals venturing down the path of innovation in foreign markets. Each of the five factors is examined in turn.

R&D AND INNOVATION ABROAD

Before turning to insights gleaned from the survey, a few general observations about the role of R&D in the innovative process are in order.

First, new technologies or products do not spring full-born, like Pallas Athena, from the forehead of Zeus; rather, they are the result of patient, thorough, and often expensive R&D efforts. This R&D sometimes requires investigation into disparate fields of both the basic and applied sciences, and establishing such an R&D facility is no simple matter that can be achieved overnight. It may require outlay of substantial capital for equipment alone, to which must be added the cost of staffing it with the best available personnel, and so forth.

Second, embodied in the overall organization's structure, whether parent or subsidiary, must be stable, ongoing support for the proinnovation R&D process. Also necessary are channels of communication, either formal or informal, that permit both the requirements and results of R&D to be integrated into the various other activities of the corporation. Both conditions are evolutionary in nature, in part because issues of control and structure in a corporation are highly sensitive matters and in part because the focus of proinnovation R&D tends to change over time.

One approach to assessing a U.S. multinational's likelihood of innovating abroad is to compare highly R&D-intensive multinationals (those that allocate 3 percent or more of total sales to R&D) with moderately R&D-intensive multinationals (1 to 3 percent). Does intensity of R&D correlate with a tendency to innovate abroad?

Several additional general observations about R&D are pertinent here:

First, recalling the discussion in Chapter 2, those U.S. multinationals that historically have had secure technology monopolies abroad are rarely highly R&D intensive.

Second, the more a U.S. firm spends on R&D, the more likely it is to produce innovations than one with less of an R&D commitment.[1] As discussed earlier, these innovations then may establish valuable technology monopolies until domestic and foreign competitors enter the market. A continual series of innovations may allow highly R&D-intensive multinationals to perpetuate technology monopolies in both domestic and foreign markets far beyond their normal expected lifespan.

Third, moderately R&D-intensive multinationals rarely de-

Table 3.1
Relation between R&D Intensity and Foreign Innovations by
U.S. Multinationals from 1970–1979

R&D Intensity	Number of R&D-Intensive Firms in Sample		
	Innovators	Non-Innovators	Total
Moderate	10	8	18
High	5	7	12
Total	15	15	30

Sources: Author survey supplemented with data from company annual reports and 1979 10K forms

velop innovations to replace maturing products.[2] As a logical consequence, they tend more frequently to experience declining technology monopolies as maturing technologies spread to domestic and foreign competitors.

Fourth, despite the siting of many R&D facilities abroad, U.S. multinationals still tend to devote a preponderance of their R&D funds in the United States; Dubin calculates this figure to be 69 percent for all U.S. multinationals.[3] Similarly, the *types* of R&D are differentiated between domestic and foreign; that is, in the United States, firms spend more on basic research, whereas in foreign markets, R&D laboratories spend more on engineering processes and on further developing existing product lines. However, there are exceptions; for instance, even in basic research, some multinationals have established R&D facilities in areas abroad where specialties in technology and science are located (particularly Switzerland and the Far East).

The survey distinguished three classes of R&D intensity: low (below 1 percent of total sales allocated to R&D), medium (1 to 3 percent), and high (above 3 percent). Table 3.1 illustrates the relationship between R&D intensity and the tendency to innovate abroad. Of the sixty multinationals surveyed, none of the thirty with low R&D expenditures innovated abroad; of the remaining thirty moderately and highly R&D-intensive firms, half did and half did not.[4]

What are the ramifications of R&D intensity on innovating abroad? Do highly R&D-intensive multinationals that outperform moderately-intensive firms in domestic innovations, outperform them abroad as well? Intuition leads one to answer in the affirmative, but the answer here is just the opposite of what intuition might suggest. There is a logical reason for this, as follows. Moderately R&D-intensive firms, which innovate less vigorously in domestic markets and which subsequently are less secure in their technology monopolies, thus are more vulnerable to competition in foreign markets. It follows that this group is more likely to take the defensive action of innovating abroad than are highly R&D-intensive firms.

This contention is modestly supported by examining the thirty R&D-intensive firms from the survey. Table 3.1 shows that ten out of eighteen (56 percent) moderately R&D-intensive firms innovated abroad, while only a slightly lower proportion of highly R&D-intensive firms (five out of twelve, or 42 percent) did so; however, the absence of a clear-cut correlation does not necessarily invalidate the hypothesis above. R&D intensity may not be an effective measure of foreign innovation for several reasons.

First, different companies direct R&D expenditures to wholly different types of R&D activities. For example, duPont expends more money on basic R&D for breakthrough innovations than does National Distillers, although both expend about the same percentage of total sales on R&D activities. Thus, R&D as a percentage of sales may reflect distinct and uncorrelatable factors.

Second, firms may allocate R&D expenditures to certain product lines disproportionately to the percentage of sales accounted for by those product lines. For example, in 1979 ITT spent 5 percent of its total U.S. sales on R&D, but much of this was devoted to its instrumentation division, which accounted for only 12 percent of total ITT sales.[5] In such instances a multinational would be counted as being highly R&D-intensive when, in actual fact, an innovation involved only a moderately R&D-intensive effort.

Although R&D may be an imprecise measure of technology monopoly, it does correlate directly with a firm's technological strength, and technological strength acts as a barrier to entry by competitors.[6]

Both moderately and highly R&D-intensive U.S. multinationals are technically oriented, and their approach to innovating abroad is consistent with their domestic strategies. That is, innovating in domestic markets is a well-understood process that can be applied to markets abroad through foreign subsidiaries.[7] Low R&D-intensive multinationals, on the other hand, lack such technical orientation and only poorly understand the process of innovating in either domestic or foreign markets. Hence, they are unlikely to innovate abroad and drop from the discussion.

All sixty multinationals surveyed spent the lion's share of their R&D budgets in the United States: Averaged for 1979, they expended approximately 85 percent of their R&D budgets in the United States, and only 15 percent in foreign countries.[8] Although some multinationals, such as Exxon and IBM, expended a greater relative percentage of their R&D budgets on foreign subsidiaries, they still gear the bulk of R&D for U.S. markets.

As might be expected, concentrating R&D activities in the United States limits the degree of technical orientation that foreign subsidiaries can gain. An anecdote illustrates:

A U.S.–based chemical company with subsidiaries throughout the world sponsored a planning meeting of all its division heads. The reports by U.S. managers differed significantly from foreign subsidiary-based managers vis-à-vis how each group approached innovation. The U.S.–based managers focused on new products under development and schedules for marketing them. The subsidiary-based managers concentrated their reports on new products developed in the U.S. and schedules for their transfer abroad.

The underlying assumption in the meeting was that innovation was appropriate in domestic but not in foreign operations. Although the multinational had a well-earned reputation as an innovator, only its domestically-based managers participated directly in the innovation process. Foreign-based managers concentrated on other, nontechnical aspects of corporate strategy. The point of this is to illustrate that managers of subsidiaries who have not assimilated a technical orientation by participating in the innovation process are less likely to innovate abroad than are managers who have.

One surrogate measure of a subsidiary's degree of technical orientation is the number of technology transfers it has received. This does not mean that as the number of technology transfers increases, so necessarily will a subsidiary's tendency to innovate abroad. Rather, the number plausibly serves as a substitute measure of the degree of a subsidiary's technical orientation, which is in turn a substitute measure for innovation. Managers must identify consumer needs, gauge demand, estimate manufacturing costs, learn new manufacturing processes, and so forth.[9]

Table 3.2 shows the relationship between the number of previous technology transfers and innovations abroad by the subsidiaries of all sixty U.S. multinationals surveyed. Only those subsidiaries having received at least ten technology transfers later innovated abroad. Thus, as a general measure, technical orientation appears to be a necessary precondition for a subsidiary to innovate abroad.

One bias underlying Table 3.2 should be noted. The number of prior technology transfers was calculated from the time at which the first innovation abroad was launched, which in most cases was some years before 1979. (These were mostly by Western European–based subsidiaries, probably because the economies of these countries were growth-oriented and had some history of U.S. multinational activity.) This bias thus should favor noninnovating multinationals, yet the data nevertheless support a positive correlation between the number of prior technology transfers and the tendency to innovate abroad.

Further, the number of transfers is not normalized for the length of time a subsidiary has operated abroad. It is possible, for example, that a subsidiary whose twenty technology transfers culminated in an innovation abroad could have been operating in that market for some twenty-odd years, while a subsidiary whose ten technology transfers culminated in *no* innovation abroad could have been operating in that market

Table 3.2
Relation between Prior Technology Transfers and Foreign
Innovation for Selected Subsidiaries of U.S. Multinationals

Number of prior tech-nology transfers	Innovators	Non-innovators	Total
1 - 5	0	7	7
6 - 9	0	22	22
10+	15	16	31
Totals	15	45	60

Note: For multinationals with innovations abroad, the number of technology transfers is measured from the innovating subsidiaries' inception to the point of introducing the first innovation abroad. For multinationals without innovations abroad, the greatest number of technology transfers to any subsidiary was used. In three instances where two subsidiaries of a multinational innovated abroad, the subsidiary with the lesser number of transfers was used. Thus, there are 60 subsidiaries in the table—one from each firm in the survey. This approach was used in order to focus on the minimum number of technology transfers necessary for foreign innovation.
Source: Survey

for only ten years. In such cases, there is no way to separate the potentially crucial effects of technology transfers and length of operating experience abroad.

However, the potential for a direct correlation between technology transfers and length of operating experience abroad is minimal. The survey data show that most subsidiaries, regardless of whether or not they innovated, began operations at least *fifteen years* prior to 1979. Indeed, most managers reported in follow-on interviews that they consider fifteen years in markets abroad to be slight with respect to innovation. Thus, normalizing the number of transfers by the number of years abroad could be misleading.

Table 3.3

Relation between Percentage of International Sales and Foreign Innovations for U.S. Multinationals

Percentage of International Sales*		Innovators	Noninnovators	Total
Less than 25%		1	18	19
25% or greater		14	27	41
	Total	15	45	60

*Defined as the ratio of sales abroad, excluding exports, to total sales.

Source: Survey

INNOVATION AND PRIOR COMMITMENT TO INTERNATIONAL GROWTH

Some U.S. multinationals are more vulnerable to competition in foreign markets than others. Multinationals that have international growth objectives are more likely to identify such threats and respond to them by innovating abroad than are multinationals having a primarily domestic growth strategy. Managers who consider foreign markets to be of only tertiary importance logically are unlikely to allocate valuable resources to them.

Likewise, not all U.S. multinationals with international growth strategies place equal emphasis on markets abroad. One handy surrogate measure of a firm's commitment to international growth strategy is the ratio of total to international sales. Table 3.3 divides the sixty firms into two groups—those having international sales less than 25 percent of total sales, and those having international sales of 25 percent or greater.

Multinationals under 25 percent stand to lose less market share to foreign competition and consequently earn less profit than those having 25 percent and above,[10] implying a "passive disincentive" to innovate abroad; however, even if these multinationals did wish to innovate abroad, several major obstacles would stand in their way.

First, these multinationals generally lack the supportive organizational structure and technical skills needed to innovate successfully abroad. Establishing such a structure or building such skills is likely to require that firm to encounter a higher cost structure than competitors already-in-place. Associated problems would increase the inherent uncertainties of innovating, such as the fact that managers and technicians would be working together for the first time, a relationship historically fraught with problems.[11]

Second, lacking the motivation of substantial sales abroad to innovate, it follows that the multinationals would have little substantive knowledge of foreign demand characteristics, market-specific conditions, how to conduct R&D for innovation abroad, and so forth. Thus, this group generally lacks both the motivation and the experience necessary to innovate abroad.

In contrast, U.S. multinationals that have relatively high percentages of international sales indeed do innovate abroad more frequently, as shown in Table 3.3. Only one of the nineteen firms having international sales of less than 25 percent innovated abroad, whereas fully fourteen of forty-one firms having sales of 25 percent or greater did innovate abroad.

This does not necessarily mean that multinationals with lesser percentages of sales will *never* innovate abroad. For instance, GM managers in 1978–79 projected greater opportunities for growth in international than in U.S. or Canadian markets; based on this projection, they allocated a disproportionately high share of resources to those international markets than they had in the past. R. M. Estes, president of GM, defined the rationale behind this shift in strategy as follows:

Recognizing the potential for growth in overseas automotive markets, General Motors recently made organizational changes to strengthen our ability to compete successfully in them. The major result of that reorganization is the closer alignment of our domestic and overseas operations in every aspect of our business: design, engineering, manufacturing, assembly, purchasing, finance, and marketing the final product.

The fact that we are now working on additional "world car" designs at General Motors reflects, in a small way, the kind of international cooperation which we must achieve within General Motors to meet the economic challenges ahead. This is true not only of GM as an individual worldwide company, but of the United States as a worldwide trader.[12]

The point should not be taken lightly: Although by and large a U.S. multinational will innovate abroad only when a substantial portion of overseas sales are at risk (a defensive reaction), it is beginning to happen that some U.S. multinationals, having identified new (and major) market opportunities abroad, will devote considerable resources and effort to innovating for those markets (a proactive strategy).

SIZE OF FIRMS

What of the relationship between the size of multinationals (measured in total 1979 assets) and the tendency to innovate abroad?

Two rationales favor larger over smaller U.S. multinationals as innovators abroad. The first of these reasons is that as multinationals increase in *financial* strength, so will their likelihood of innovating, for two reasons.[13] First, they will have greater resources with which to underwrite the expenses of establishing, staffing, and equipping an R&D and/or manufacturing facility (and thus to gain organizational economies of scale), and second, if an innovative endeavor fails, they will be more able to absorb the concomitant financial losses. Smaller, financially less strong multinationals would not enjoy these advantages.

The second rationale reasons that larger firms tend more to develop incremental than breakthrough innovations.[14] Having more highly formalized, bureaucratically oriented structures, they hence are likely to gear strategies to task-oriented, risk-averse efforts, a category to which incremental innovations belong. Since most innovations abroad are indeed incremental

Table 3.4
Asset Size Correlated with Innovation Abroad for 60 U.S.
Multinationals

Types of Firms	Number of Firms Less Than the Median	Number of Firms Greater Than the Median	Total
Innovators	7	8	15
Noninnovators	22	23	45
Total	29	31	60

Source: Survey

in nature, it follows that larger firms innovate abroad more frequently than do smaller.

However, other studies suggest that smaller firms may generate more innovations abroad, for other reasons.[15] Since smaller firms are more efficient innovators, they may perceive opportunities for growth abroad via innovations as being less uncertain. Further, they may innovate abroad for other reasons, such as their perceived vulnerability to larger firms or their lack of such intangible assets as brand-name recognition.

Survey data do not conclusively resolve this issue. Table 3.4 compares asset sizes of innovators with noninnovators, but approximately as many multinationals above the median size report innovating abroad as do multinationals below the median. However, since the survey draws only from multinationals that belong to the *Fortune* 500, the sample range may be too narrow to yield any distinct correlation between firm size and innovation abroad.

Size differences among firms in *different* industries also may obscure the relative effects of size on innovation abroad. For instance, GTE has ten times the assets of Dana, an automobile parts manufacturer. Because large firms *within* industries may possess greater organizational economies of scale and financial strength than do smaller firms, the following hypothesis is plausible: Larger firms within industries will innovate abroad

Table 3.5

Relation between Foreign Innovation and Relative Firm Size within Selected Industries

Industry	Relative Asset Size Innovators	Noninnovators
Glass	1.2	.8
Chemicals	1.3	.7
Computers	1.3	.8
Machinery	1.1	.9
Rubber	1.1	.9

Note: Relative asset size is compared with average asset size of firms within each industry with at least one innovation abroad. Relative size is determined by dividing the average of firms within specific industries into asset size of specific firms.

Source: Survey

more frequently than will smaller firms within the same industries.

The fact that some companies have multiple product lines further complicates the analysis. ITT is typical. ITT designates telecommunications as its primary industry more for historical reasons than because it is, in actuality, its main business activity. In fact, the corporation sprawls across numerous product lines. Lacking data with which to quantify the relative sizes of firms' product lines by sales, assets, or contributions to earnings, any comparison of firms in the same industries is not likely to bear fruit. For example, one of ITT's subsidiaries developed a disc brake in Germany, but absent specific data on its size, ITT's innovating subsidiary cannot be compared accurately with other firms in the same industry.

Subject to these qualifications, Table 3.5 depicts five industries in which at least one firm innovated abroad and one did not. The table indicates that larger firms within industries tend more to innovate abroad. In three of the five industries (chemicals, machinery, and rubber), two or more firms reported innovations abroad. Each innovating firm exceeded the mean size of firms in its respective industry.

SUMMARY

This section has analyzed the effects of R&D intensity, international sales, and firm size on innovation abroad. U.S. multinationals that innovate abroad tend to combine the three factors most optimally in the following way: They are highly R&D-intensive, have a significant portion (25 + percent) of sales abroad, and are larger than other firms in their respective industries. It is impossible, however, to separate out the individual effects of each variable. Is the largest firm in an industry, with 20 percent of international sales, more or less likely to innovate abroad than a smaller firm in the same industry with 40 percent of international sales? The available data do not indicate an answer. It is clear, however, that all three elements combined are necessary to spur innovation abroad.

EXPERIENCE AND STRUCTURE: IMPACT ON INNOVATING

Having quantified in general terms three factors crucial to successful innovating abroad, the following section now examines two less quantifiable factors. The first is length of prior experience operating abroad. Experience is perceived to reduce uncertainties in four general areas: market, political, technical, and personnel. The second is the impact of a parent structuring its organization along an international division, product lines or geographical area orientation.

Experience Abroad

Common sense suggests that multinationals with less operating experience abroad would tend to innovate abroad less than those having greater experience, and Table 3.6 supports

Table 3.6

**Relation between Experience Abroad and Foreign Innovation
for Selected Subsidiaries of U.S. Multinationals**

Experience Abroad by Years	Innovators	Noninnovators	Total
Less than 10 years	0	16	16
10 years or more	15	29	44
Total	15	45	60

Note: For multinationals with innovations abroad, experience is
measured as the number of years innovating subsidiaries
operate abroad. For multinationals without innovations abroad,
experience is measured as the number of years the oldest
subsidiaries of each firm operated abroad. In the three
instances where two subisdiaries of a multinational innovated
abroad, the subsidiary with the lesser number of years abroad
was used. Thus, there are 60 subsidiaries in the table, one
from each firm in the survey.

Source: Survey

this. *None* of the multinationals whose subsidiaries had less
than ten years experience abroad undertook innovations
abroad, whereas fifteen of the forty-four firms with ten or more
years of experience did. Thus, only multinationals with subsidiaries experienced in markets abroad innovated in those
markets.

Two observations about Table 3.6, both relating to how
length of experience is measured, support the contention that
less experienced firms tend to innovate abroad less frequently.
The measure of experience abroad for noninnovators spans the
time from which the oldest subsidiary began operating up
through 1979. The measure for innovators includes only the
time from the start up of a subsidiary abroad and the introduction of an innovation, both occurring prior to 1979.

First, this measurement means that noninnovators have had
a longer time to accumulate experience than those multinationals with subsidiaries that launched innovations before
1979. Hence, a noninnovating subsidiary would have accumulated more experience than a subsidiary that started in the
same year and innovated before 1979.

Second, it may be argued that certain market factors may motivate innovation regardless of a subsidiary's experience. Because incentives to innovate in foreign markets have been increasing steadily over time, the noninnovators would have found market incentives greater during the 1970s than would those experienced firms that innovated in the late 1960s. The absence of innovations by inexperienced firms during the 1970s suggests that experience does, in fact, influence the decision to innovate abroad.

Actual operating experience can lessen uncertainty in four major areas: market, political, technical, and labor. As these uncertainties are lessened, the motivation for innovating abroad should increase.

Market Uncertainty. The U.S. market is littered with products that perished at the hands of misjudged demand, a misfortune not limited just to small start-up entrepreneurial firms. For example, duPont devoted over $100 million developing a synthetic shoe leather (CORFAM™), but despite voluminous and optimistic data on expected demand in the U.S. market, CORFAM flopped.[16] And if there are market uncertainties in the United States, whose consumers are among the most thoroughly tested, tabulated, and wooed in the world, then the problem might be ten- or twentyfold in markets abroad.

For example, do many Japanese women drive automobiles, and if they do, is it they or their husbands who decide which brand to buy? The Chinese associate the color white with mourning; will that affect the market for coffee (or tea) creamer? For refined sugar? For disposable diapers?

Religious, cultural, economic, and historic factors all influence foreign consumer preferences in ways no U.S.–based marketing department can anticipate. Such uncertainty can be lethal to an innovation, and the only surefire remedy is through hard-core, hands-on experience in the host country. One way to reduce such uncertainty is to establish managers in subsidiaries abroad drawn from the host-country population.

By no means are market uncertainties confined to customer imponderables. Even more significant are market supply and price conditions of raw materials, the transportation infrastructure to deliver them, and the availability, proximity, and reliability of intermediary industries to transform these raw materials into a form usable by the subsidiary. An antiquated railway system in the Rajasthan province of northern India might severely influence the economic feasibility of both importing raw goods and distributing finished products. Likewise, disruptions in oil supplies due to OPEC intervention, hostilities in the Persian Gulf area, and other events would render energy supplies and prices insecure for subsidiaries based in countries that did not have substitutable fuels readily accessible.

Whereas host-country demand uncertainties can be ameliorated by hiring experienced nationals as subsidiary managers, the larger market uncertainties discussed above yield to no such facile solutions. Vertically integrating into supply sources of raw materials might be one tactic, but this is an expensive proposition. Intermediate measures, such as stockpiling, are usually available and more easily and inexpensively achieved. Furthermore, as a general rule, the less global an uncertainty, the more readily it should yield to the benefits of experience. For instance, within a few years a subsidiary in Malaysia should have accumulated invaluable knowledge of how monsoon conditions affect, say, transportation conditions in that country; it then can make compensatory adjustments, whether constructing port facilities or improving rail lines or gearing production activity to match the dry seasons. In any event, experience operating abroad is an invaluable tool in reducing market uncertainties, and because uncertainties are by definition unknown entities, it is only through experience that they can be reduced.

Political Uncertainty. When assessing the possible effects of political actions by U.S. federal, state, and local governments on business conditions, U.S. firms enjoy the benefit of historical experience. Even with such radical actions as government deregulation of an entire industry, the affected parties all participate in the planning process, are knowledgeable about the other actors involved, and enjoy relatively free access to pertinent information. At best, they can draw upon the experience of previously deregulated industries to gain insights into what they might reasonably expect. The value of this should not be underestimated, particularly when compared to the political uncertainties of innovating abroad.

U.S. managers rarely can assess the impact of the policies of host governments with the same degree of reliability as they can in the United States, not even in politically stable countries that have government structures similar to ours. For example, after the 1981 election of François Mitterrand in France, U.S. multinationals expressed widespread concern about the possible impacts of nationalization on their situations.

The problem is exacerbated further when managers, particularly those in U.S. corporate headquarters, do not understand foreign political structures very well. In many nondemocratic countries, managers feel that the presence of a U.S. multinational may be interpreted as a challenge to national sovereignty, and possibly used as a political tool in times of instability or conflict. Constantly hanging over U.S. multinationals operating in markets abroad is the threat that host-country governments might suddenly and unpredictably take actions opposed to the firm's well-being.[17] How can such uncertainties be mitigated?

The obvious answer again is through hands-on operating experience. The more intimately a manager knows the host country, the more likely he will be able to foresee and accurately gauge the effects of political disruptions. And a manager with highly sophisticated and extremely wide-ranging knowledge of the host country can turn that knowledge into competitive advantage relative to other U.S. and non–U.S. multinationals. The subsidiary manager, through frequent and ongoing negotiations with political entities in the host country, gains invaluable perspectives and knowledge about government attitudes, pressures, needs, and priorities, which then can be used to anticipate future actions.[18] Managers from both IBM and GTE report that they had to spend *years* dealing with host-government policymakers before they were secure in their understanding of that country's political priorities and processes.[19] Absent such "hands-on" experience, managers will attribute a high degree of uncertainty to potentially adverse political actions, and uncertainty militates against innovating.

Personnel Uncertainty. The manager of a major U.S. multinational electronics manufacturer puts it thus: "One major problem our company encounters when innovating abroad is finding the skilled labor and the engineers who have experience with even the simplest circuitry. In the United States we take such experience for granted, but in some countries overseas it is a real problem."[20]

Imagine the difficulties, not in Western Europe but in countries such as India or Brazil, where even the best and the brightest of local employees lack such fundamental knowledge. A subsidiary must have a financial department, and a financial department must have accountants, and in India, say, those accountants must be readily able to rapidly calculate daily fluctuating rupees into dollars. The skills involved are by no means trivial, and an error by an accountant in estimating the purchase price of a raw material bound in Thailand (*bahts*) and translating it first into rupees and then into dollars—such an error could have repercussions throughout both the subsidiary and the parent multinational itself.

Only through direct hands-on experience with foreign labor pools can managers of a U.S. multinational subsidiary determine how best to handle such uncertainties. Where can the best staff be drawn from? Local industries might be one source, but only experience can give a manager this knowledge. Would it be more efficient to import middle-level managers from the United States, or to train foreign nationals to do the job? In terms of practical operations the importance of these questions cannot be underestimated, and it is only through rugged and hard-won experience that the manager of a foreign subsidiary can know best how to answer them.

Summary. Although impossible to quantify, the above discussion of how experience might reduce market, political, technical, and personnel uncertainties underscores another major hazard of innovating abroad. Some experience can be "bought," in the sense of hiring consultants; and in some cases no amount of experience (say, in predicting the price of oil several years down the road) can yield useful information; however, there is a vast middle ground, and it is in this middle ground where hands-on, informed experience works best to reduce, contain, or eliminate the hazards of uncertainty. As a rule, it appears that the more distant the manager is from the problem, the more likely misjudgments are. It follows that U.S. multinationals might wisely give purview over uncertainties endemic to a host country to the managers of its subsidiary there, refraining from direct interference except in more cross-national matters.

The Importance of Organizational Structure to Innovating Abroad

As U.S. multinationals gain experience operating in foreign markets, their organizational structures tend to evolve from the more simple to the more complex, as follows. First, the U.S. multinational erects either functional departments or, less frequently, autonomous subsidiaries in the corporate headquarters. The second phase sees the creation of an international division. The third phase involves the establishment of a globally oriented structure organized either by product line or geographic area (or some mixture of both, known as a matrix).[21] A U.S. multinational geared to innovation abroad is likely to have evolved either or both of the latter two types of organizational structure.

In 1972, John Stopford and Louis T. Wells, Jr., demonstrated that R&D-intensive multinationals having diversified product lines tended to organize by product line, whereas non–R&D-intensive multinationals, which have maturing products, organized more by geographical area.[22] Since R&D-intensive multinationals tend to innovate abroad and non–R&D-intensive ones do not, it follows that those multinationals that innovate abroad should tend to organize by product line.

However, more recent research suggests an alternative hypothesis.[23] U.S. multinationals that already have established subsidiaries abroad tend to transfer their technologies to them at a demonstrably faster rate than do multinationals primarily organized either by product line or geographical area. Since the number of technology transfers tends to reflect the degree of a subsidiary's technical orientation, this is one reason that multinationals with international subsidiaries innovate

Table 3.7
Relation between Foreign Innovation and Organizational
Structure for U.S. Multinationals

Type of Organizational Structure	Innovators	Noninnovators	Totals
Geographical Area	11	18	29
Product	4	17	21
International Division	0	10	10

Note: Matrix organizations of five multinationals are included in the geographical area category since managers of each stated that they were organized by geographical area at the time of their first innovations.

Source: Survey

abroad more frequently than do multinationals with either other type of organizational structure.

Table 3.7 relates U.S. multinationals innovating abroad to their organizational structures. Contrary to expectations, foreign innovation occurs least frequently in multinationals organized by either product line or international divisions. Multinationals organized by geographic area are more inclined to innovate abroad, for several reasons.

First, the geographical area organization offers the greatest opportunities to grow. Within a given geographical market, the multinational has established multiple departments through which managers can develop an intercommunicating structure with which to administer the innovation process. Since these geographical area-oriented subsidiaries usually operate as profit centers, managers, measuring profitability, will perceive an incentive to innovate, particularly if competitors' innovations are encroaching on market share.

Further, managers of geographical area-oriented subsidiaries tend to have comparable ranking in the organizational hierarchy with their counterparts in other areas. Such managers may use their authority to advocate an innovation to corporate headquarters. This further helps to explain why multinationals with geographical area structures innovate abroad more frequently than do multinationals with product line orientations. In fact, all 14 innovations for world markets in the survey came from firms having such geographical-area structures.[24] This finding is, in part, consistent with the research of Stopford and Wells. Although they conclude that R&D-intensive multinationals tend to organize around product lines—a conclusion that favors innovations abroad by product line organizations—they also find that firms with maturing products tend to organize by geographical area.[25] As shown above, firms marketing maturing products are more likely to encounter the types of competition that induce innovations abroad.

There is an explanation for this anomaly. As products matured, R&D-intensive multinationals originally organized by product line shifted more to a geographical area orientation. (This reorganization may also reflect an attempt to reduce costs by integrating certain manufacturing and marketing functions across national borders.) As competition further intensifies after reorganization, these multinationals subsequently elect to innovate abroad. Indeed, five of the eleven innovating firms with a geographical area orientation were organized by product line prior to innovating abroad.

Organizing by product line eliminates some potential to develop the capability to innovate abroad. Although this type of organization may be fluid, its focus still tends to be on domestic markets: Of the twenty-one firms organized by product line, only seven, including the four with innovations abroad, reported international sales of 25 percent or more. By concentrating on domestic markets, the incentives to innovate and the location of managers with the authority to champion innovations tend to center in U.S. rather than in foreign markets.

The organizational structure least likely to innovate abroad is the international division. Despite evidence by Vernon and Davidson that multinationals with international divisions transfer technology at faster rates than do those with alternative forms of organization, this organizational form also centers innovative activities in the United States.[26]

The objectives of international departments are to transfer

innovations from domestic to foreign markets. This explicit strategy centered innovation champions in the United States, and channels incentives to innovate to domestic, not foreign, managers. Unlike organizations by product line, in which foreign subsidiary managers have incentives to argue for innovation to offset declining market shares, managers of international divisions typically seek only to supplement declining market shares through technology transfers to subsidiaries abroad.[27]

Multinationals with international divisions also tend to suffer from a lack of direct operating experience abroad, which also militates against innovating abroad. Of the ten firms surveyed with international divisions, only five had accumulated experience of ten years or more, and only one reported international sales of 25 percent or greater.

The survey also suggests that the international department structure tends to concentrate more of its innovative capabilities in domestic markets than do other structures. One test of the degree of domestic focus is the location of R&D labs abroad, since a multinational can hardly develop new products and processes in foreign markets without proximity to R&D labs. Table 3.8 reveals that organizations by geographical area moved R&D labs abroad more frequently and aggressively than did organizations either by product line or international divisions.

CONCLUSIONS

Drawing upon the author's survey of sixty U.S. multinationals and applicable literature, this chapter has examined the influence of five factors on a U.S. multinational's propensity to innovate abroad. Although more suggestive than conclusive, survey results indicate the following. First, highly R&D-intensive multinationals, which innovate for domestic markets more often than do moderately R&D-intensive multinationals, tend to demonstrate a greater degree of technical orientation, and technical orientation is shown to correlate positively with the tendency to innovate abroad. Second, multinationals having a greater commitment to growth in international markets (meas-

Table 3.8
Relation between Global Organizational Structures and
Foreign R&D Labs for U.S. Multinationals

Type of Organizational Structure	Foreign R&D Labs	No Foreign R&D Labs	Total
Geographical Area	24	1	25
Product	15	6	21
International Division	3	7	10
Totals	42	14	56

Note: Of the 60 multinationals surveyed, 4 noninnovators did not respond
on this subject.

Source: Survey

ured in terms of foreign to total sales) stand to lose more to
competitors abroad, and hence will tend to innovate abroad
more frequently. Third, although evidence is not conclusive, it
appears that larger multinationals, at least within the same
industries, tend to innovate abroad more often than do smaller
firms.

The chapter then examined two other factors: the influences
of past operating experience abroad and of the parent corporation's structure. Experience is shown to lessen uncertainty
in four vital areas: market, politics, technology, and personnel.
The lessening of uncertainty correlates positively with the
tendency to innovate abroad. Finally, U.S. multinationals may
organize for activity in foreign markets along one of three structures: international division, geographical area, or product
line. Evidence demonstrates that those multinationals organized by geographical area moved R&D laboratories abroad
more aggressively than did those organized either by international division or product lines. Given the importance of
R&D abroad to innovate in foreign markets, it follows that
organizing by geographical area is more conducive to innovating abroad than either of the other two approaches.

NOTES

1. Stopford and Wells, pp. 3–21; and Robert B. Stobaugh, Jr., and Sidney M. Robbins, *Money in the Multinational Enterprise: A Study in Financial Policy* (New York: Basic Books, 1973), pp. 37–137.

2. Raymond Vernon, *Storm Over the Multinationals: The Real Issues* (Cambridge, Mass.: Harvard University Press, 1977), pp. 103–38, 175–90.

3. Dubin.

4. The measure of R&D intensity used here is the same as that used by the National Science Foundation (NSF) for compilation of R&D statistics for U.S. companies. See National Science Foundation, *Science Indicators (various years), Report of the National Science Board* (Washington, D.C.: U.S. Government Printing Office, stock no. 038–000–00341–1 [for 1976]), pp. 1–41. NSF data cluster R&D expenditures by U.S. companies into three categories: Low R&D intensity is defined as 1 percent or less of total sales; medium intensity, between 1 and 3 percent; and high, 3 percent or greater. Many other researchers have used these categories in their work. For instance, see F. M. Scherer, *Industrial Market Structure and Economic Performance* (Chicago: Rand McNally College Publishing Co., 1970), p. 359. Other researchers have found R&D levels to differ significantly from those reported by the NSF. For example, see Raymond Vernon and William H. Davidson, "Foreign Production of Technology-Intensive Products by U.S.–based Multinational Enterprises, "Harvard University Graduate School of Business, Paper no. 79–5 (Boston, 1979), Appendix. The difference appears to derive from the differences in sample populations. The NSF uses industrywide averages, whereas other researchers use data from selected multinationals. Since multinationals tend to expend more on R&D activities than does the average firm in the industry in which they operate, one would expect the industry average to be lower.

5. Author interview with General Motors manager, proprietary.

6. See, for example, Raymond Vernon, "Organization as a Scale Factor in the Growth of Firms," in J. W. Markham and G. F. Papanek, eds., *Industrial Organization and Economic Development* (Boston: Houghton-Mifflin Co., 1970); Jesse W. Markham, "Market Structure, Business Conduct, and Innovation," in *American Economic Review,* May 1965, p. 325; and John Kenneth Galbraith, *The New Industrial State* (Boston: Houghton-Mifflin Co., 1967), p. 4.

7. The concept that U.S. multinationals would prefer to use their domestic markets as a base for a change in strategy stems in part

from the notion that managers are averse to the uncertainty. For example, see Donald A. Schon, *Technology and Change* (New York: Delacorte Press, 1967), pp. 19–111; Raymond Vernon, *Sovereignty at Bay: The Multinational Spread of U.S. Enterprises* (New York: Basic Books, 1971), pp. 3–25, 60–112; Christopher Freeman, *The Economics of Industrial Innovation* (Baltimore: Penguin Books, 1974), pp. 74–107; William J. Abernathy and James M. Utterback, "Innovation and the Evolving Structure of the Firm," Harvard University Graduate School of Business Paper no. 75–18 (Boston, June 1975), pp. 1–31; and H. Igor Ansoff and John M. Stewart, "Strategies for a Technology-based Business," in *Harvard Business Review,* November/December 1967, reprint.

Much evidence indicates that multinationals tend to pursue similar strategies in both domestic and foreign markets. For example, see James Brian Quinn, "Technology Transfer by Multinational Companies," in *Harvard Business Review,* November/December 1969, reprint; Vernon, *Sovereignty at Bay,* pp. 66–122; Vernon, *Storm over the Multinationals,* pp. 39–58; Vernon and Davidson, "Foreign Production," pp. 33–62; and William H. Gruber, Dileep Mehta, and Raymond Vernon, "The R&D Factor in International Trade and International Investment in U.S. Industries," in Louis T. Wells, ed., *The Product Life Cycle and International Trade* (Boston: Harvard University Graduate School of Business Administration, Division of Research, 1972), pp. 111–39.

8. As suggested in note 4 above, data on the issue of U.S. multinational R&D expenditures in foreign countries differ depending upon source used. The author's survey found that U.S. multinationals having R&D laboratories sited in foreign countries allocated approximately 15 percent of their total R&D budgets to those laboratories, on average. For other estimates, see John H. Dunning, "Technology, United States Investment, and European Economic Growth," in Charles P. Kindleberger (ed.), *The International Corporation* (Cambridge, Mass.: MIT Press, 1970), pp. 162–63; and Nasrullah S. Fatemi, Gail W. Williams, and Tribaut de Sait-Phalle, *Multinational Corporations* (New York: A. S. Barnes and Company, 1975), p. 125.

9. See Robert Ronstadt, *Research and Development Abroad by U.S. Multinationals* (New York: Praeger Publishers, 1977), pp. 61–127; and Dunning, "Technology," pp. 141–76.

10. See Scherer, *Industrial Market Structure,* pp. 346–78. Percentage of international to total sales appears to be a more accurate measure of a U.S. multinational's commitment to an international strategy than other potentially plausible measures, such as total as-

sets of number of personnel employed in foreign markets, as follows: Sales are stated in current dollars, whereas assets may be stated at historical costs. Use of personnel figures would assume both that capital/labor ratios and quality of work are identical in both foreign and domestic markets; evidence militates against such an assumption.

11. See Vernon, *Storm over the Multinationals,* pp. 59–87, 110–114; Robert B. Stobaugh, Jr., "How to Analyze Foreign Investment Climates," in *Harvard Business Review,* September/October 1969, pp. 100–108; Freeman, *The Economics of Industrial Innovation,* pp. 253–82; William J. Abernathy and Balaji S. Chakravarthy, "Government Intervention and Innovation in Industry: A Policy Framework," Harvard University Graduate School of Business Paper no. 78–4 (Boston, 1978); Raymond Vernon, *The Economic and Political Consequences of Multinational Enterprise, An Anthology* (Boston: Harvard University Graduate School of Business Administration, Division of Research, 1972), pp. 23–42, 205–236; and Vernon, "Organization as a Scale Factor in the Growth of Firms."

12. R. M. Estes, Reprint of speech, September 20, 1979, General Motors Corporation.

13. For example, see Vernon, "Organization as a Scale Factor;" Markham, "Market Structure," p. 325; and Galbraith, *The New Industrial State,* p. 4.

14. See Scherer, *Industrial Market Structure,* pp. 352–362; and J. Jewkes, D. Sawers, and R. Stillman, *The Sources of Invention* (New York: St. Martin's Press, 1959).

15. For two views on this point, see Arthur Gerstenfeld, *Innovation: A Study of Technological Policy* (Washington, D.C.: University Press of America, 1977), pp. 82–88; and Arnold C. Cooper, "R&D Is More Efficient in Small Companies," in *Harvard Business Review,* May/June 1964, reprint.

16. Author's interview with manager at duPont, proprietary.

17. For example, see Vernon, *Sovereignty at Bay,* pp. 60–112; Stephen H. Robock, "Political Risk: Identification and Assessment," in *Columbia Journal of World Business,* August 1971, pp. 6–20; and Kenneth N. Waltz, "The Myth of National Interdependence," in Kindleberger, *The International Corporation,* pp. 205–223.

18. Robert B. Stobaugh, Jr., "Where in the World Should We Put That Plant?" *Harvard Business Review,* January/February 1969, pp. 132–33; John H. Dunning, "Technology Transfer," in Kindleberger, *The International Corporation,* pp. 160–63; Fatemi et al., *Multinational Corporations,* pp. 100–127; and author's interviews with managers of various U.S. multinationals, proprietary.

19. Author's interviews with managers at IBM and GTE, proprietary.

20. Author's interview with manager of a U.S. multinational, proprietary.

21. For a clear model of the evolution of multinationals, see Stopford and Wells, pp. 3–29. Other examples may be found in A. Perlmutter, "The Torturous Evolution of the Multinational Corporation," in David W. Ewing, ed., *Technological Change and Management* (Cambridge, Mass.: Harvard University Press, 1970); and E. G. Woodroufe, "Technology and Business Opportunity for the International Business," in Ewing, *Technological Change and Management,* pp. 87–107. As multinationals' global structures evolve, the organization of their subsidiaries usually undergoes changes in the direction of assuming greater responsibilities. For example, see Stobaugh and Robbins, *Money in the Multinational Enterprise;* and Ronstadt, *Research and Development Abroad.*

22. Stopford and Wells, pp. 30–47, 63–84.

23. Vernon and Davidson, "Foreign Production," pp. 57–62.

24. The author's findings are consistent with those of other researchers. For example, see Gilbert H. Clee and Wilbur M. Sachtjen, "Organizing a Worldwide Business," in *Harvard Business Review,* November/December 1964, reprint.

25. Stopford and Wells, pp. 30–47, 63–84.

26. See Clee and Sachtjen, "Organizing a Worldwide Business;" and Vernon and Davidson, "Foreign Production."

27. Derived from author's interviews with managers of various U.S. multinationals, proprietary.

4

The Movement from a Defensive to a Proactive Strategy

At least since 1984, U.S. multinationals have begun to reassess the role innovation might play in extending, recapturing, or creating new foreign markets threatened, eroded, or outright lost to competitors. In point of fact, the past several years have seen the beginning of what may become a radical shift in basic U.S. multinational strategy: reliance upon innovation abroad as the crucial strategic tool in markets abroad. Indeed, many multinationals have moved from viewing innovation as being an exotic, risky, or wholly unnecessary undertaking, to regarding it—in some instances with open arms—as a viable option, even when this entails a restructuring of some corporate priorities. One manager illustrates the shift in attitudes as follows:

When we first started developing new products for foreign markets, the fear was sometimes palpable in corporate corridors; it was thick enough to chew on. There were so many things that could go wrong, so much room for misjudgments. We had only the sketchiest idea of the levels of technology or of the technological competence of managers in foreign markets. We had only the barest-bones idea of how we, or they, would organize to cope with our innovations. It was like sex the first time, all trepidation and clumsiness and no grace. But we were fast learners, we shed our inhibitions the more we learned, and it all happened pretty fast. Now, today, if one of our subsidiaries makes a pitch to headquarters to support an innovation, and if they justify it, back it up with enough concrete information, we might just rush in where once angels feared to tread.[1]

As the above quote suggests, the shift to a strategy of innovating abroad was to some extent evolutionary. That is, "innovations" abroad first involved extensions or refinements of existing product lines. Over time, this process was repeated again and again, increasing in complexity and sophistication. And, as interviews with managers of all fifteen innovating multinationals indicate, all have broadened the scope of their innovative activities. Now, rather than simply extending or transferring existing technologies or products, some U.S. multinationals are using their subsidiaries abroad to develop entirely *new* products, and in some cases even establishing entrepreneurial-modeled units to support them.

As might be expected, such an approach to innovation abroad involves more sophisticated personnel and greater depth of organizational commitment than before. Thus, some subsidiaries are now structured as virtually "stand-alone" units, although at present these are more the exception than the rule, and many foreign subsidiaries are directly responsible for recruiting a broad spectrum of employees (technicians, accountants, marketing staff, and so forth) without direct influence of their parent companies. The trend appears to be to grant these subsidiaries increasing independence as they develop the skills and knowledge needed to operate effectively in their foreign-based markets. Further, integrating a proinnovation orientation into the parent company's planning process is increasingly regarded as critical to success abroad. The goal now is to identify *new* business opportunities in markets abroad, rather than viewing foreign markets solely in terms of a lag in demand over U.S. markets.

FROM A DEFENSIVE TO A PROACTIVE STRATEGY

As we have seen, past defensive reactions have progressed from simple technology transfers abroad in support of exported products, to establishing first manufacturing and then R&D support facilities overseas. Innovations developed for U.S. markets were first transferred abroad, then modified to meet the specific demand characteristics of those markets, and finally manufactured and marketed through subsidiaries based overseas. The logical next step in this progression is to innovate specifically and explicitly for foreign markets, drawing upon resources already in place, whether they be R&D, technological, financial, manufacturing, marketing, or structural, and to shore up those resources and resolve other weaknesses as needed, all to serve the tricky business of innovation.

This heralds a significant shift in fundamental strategy. Rather than merely reacting to competitive threats, some U.S. multinationals now are moving more to a *proactive*—or even preemptive—approach. Of the fifteen innovating multinationals, thirteen incorporated the development and marketing of new products or technologies in the long-range strategies of both parent companies and their subsidiaries. It is notable that the process actively involves the *managers* of those subsidiaries, whose input is crucial to identifying future business opportunities. Managers of subsidiaries, beginning around the mid–1970s, were for the first time becoming a key resource. Some subsidiaries were being infused with the same entrepreneurial management styles once reserved exclusively for domestic corporate headquarters and for small start-up entrepreneurial firms here in the United States.

There is a basic advantage to shifting the innovation emphasis to the subsidiary. Subsidiary managers are more likely to develop new products equal or superior to those the parent is developing or marketing in foreign markets. U.S. multinationals that rely on the input of such managers tend to develop strategies that meet competition abroad head-on, rather than to engage in border scrimmages for market share. And part of this strategy involves parent multinationals helping ensure that their subsidiary managers gain parity in managerial competence, entrepreneurial dexterity, and technological skill with those of their competitors.

Rather than merely transferring technologies or such tangible assets as capital goods and production equipment, parent multinationals now are transferring intangible assets as well. Given the high level of technological and marketing skills now possessed by U.S., non–U.S., and even national firms in many world markets, the transfer of intangible assets seems an eventual inevitability. However true this may be, it is notable that intangible assets are the last type of asset a U.S. multinational transfers to subsidiaries abroad, for several reasons.

First, in many cases a U.S. multinational has underwritten R&D, manufacturing, marketing, and other activities to develop a given technology. So long as that multinational holds either a monopolistic or oligopolistic advantage in a foreign market, and demand for its product is secure, managers perceive no need to innovate. In such event, there is no directly apparent motivation to transfer intangible assets.

However, monopolistic or oligopolistic advantages change over time, and when they do, incentives to innovate may change. Large, traditional U.S. multinationals can no longer assume that their newly developed products will succeed as frequently, as well, or for as long as when there were fewer competitors. A good example is U.S. computer software companies; a spreadsheet program geared to a specific market segment may be superseded by another virtually overnight. This fact is true to a lesser degree in foreign markets, however, where new technologies are being developed at a lower rate than in U.S. markets. This implies that there are greater opportunities for subsidiaries to exploit a new product abroad, and thus parent U.S. multinationals may see motivations to gear innovations specifically for foreign markets, whereas they might be constrained by market "glut" from doing so for U.S. consumption.

These are very different from post–World War II conditions, when products developed for U.S. consumption were quickly exported to markets abroad and motivations to innovate specifically for foreign markets at first were virtually nonexistent. Foreign markets were riddled with uncertainties, cultural differences and legal and business practices poorly understood, managers unproven, government policies in perplexing flux, labor populations less technologically skilled and less affluent than in the United States, and so forth. Also militating against a proactive approach to innovating abroad was the enormity of a U.S. market that seemed, particularly in the 1950s and early 1960s, to be insatiable in its appetite for innovations, whether they be chrome fins on cars or wringer washers or styrofoam cups.

These conditions began to change, however, and in time the once high cost of innovating for foreign markets became more comparable with innovating for U.S. markets. First, commercial success by a U.S. firm in the U.S. market became less assured as numerous competitors, both domestic and foreign, entered these markets and exploited available advantages. Second, other U.S. firms began encroaching on foreign markets once considered to be the exclusive purview of a given U.S. firm. Third, as other U.S. and non–U.S. multinationals and national firms entered markets abroad, and as a host of country-specific internal factors changed, so did the demand characteristics of those markets. And fourth, as management and technical skills began emerging abroad, certain uncertainties were lowered for competitors, which in turn altered the conditions of U.S. multinationals' relative competitive advantage.

Despite these changes in the world business environment, the following should be borne in mind. Any innovative activity tends to be risky; it follows that transferring an innovative (or entrepreneurial) activity abroad involves a high degree of risk. However, if the transfer abroad of the innovative approach is perceived as being strategically necessary, then there is a logical way to lower those risks, as follows. If transferring tangible assets abroad is a first step in establishing innovation abroad, then it surely follows that it is less risky to transfer these to subsidiaries that are experienced in innovation. And since experience resides in large part in the hands of managers, it also follows that the best people to train proinnovation subsidiary managers are U.S. multinational personnel themselves experienced in U.S. markets.

At the same time U.S. managers were seeing the necessity and opportunity for entrepreneurship in U.S. markets, two changes were underway abroad. First, non–U.S. multinationals and, to a lesser extent, national firms were gaining the technological know-how, managerial professionalism, and labor skills equal or superior to those of the United States. This resulted in part from technology transfers, and not necessarily those from U.S. multinationals but from a growing number of non–U.S. multinationals as well. Each technology transfer increases the foreign manager's skillfulness, knowledge, and technical expertise. He gains in his ability to manage R&D facilities for innovation, to establish control systems (see Chapter 5), to use marketing know-how, and so forth. As James Brian Quinn suggests, this process was *evolutionary,* with foreign managers gaining innovative expertise in increments.[2] The process holds both for managers of U.S. and non–U.S. subsidiaries, and to a lesser extent, of national firms.

The entrepreneurial "spirit" is by no means singularly a U.S. phenomenon; rather, it pervades all countries, all peoples and all cultures. After World War II through the mid–1970s, circumstances conducive to proactive innovation abroad were relatively absent for U.S. multinationals, but as technologies changed and non–U.S. firms began gaining experience, the differences in experiential levels began to diminish. Thus, when IBM established a computer R&D facility in Switzerland in order to draw upon the experience of Swiss computer scientists, the Japanese soon followed suit. It was often true that non–U.S. firms took the lead in proactively innovating in foreign markets. The point is that as entrepreneurial skills, managerial competency, and technical acumen spread to all classes of firms doing business overseas, so too did *motivations* to innovate abroad.

At the same time however, there were several important factors that *inhibited* U.S. multinationals from innovating abroad. So long as U.S. multinationals held an oligopoly's position in foreign markets and demand for their products was strong, managers would hardly incur the cost of developing innovative products or processes abroad, particularly given the uncertainty of foreign markets. The return was unknown and the risk high. So long as foreign markets purchased the goods developed from technologies developed in the United States, U.S. multinationals could earn as large or larger a return from transfer of domestically developed technologies as from foreign technologies. Particularly when these technologies can be transferred to U.S. multinational subsidiaries at low cost, there would have to be substantial increases in demand and returns in order to justify the higher costs of developing new products abroad.

In addition, so long as U.S. multinationals held technology monopolies, belonged to oligopolies, and focused R&D activities in the United States, few U.S. managers would be willing to upset the oligopolist structure by innovating abroad. Their desire to maintain oligopolist stability led them to anchor R&D efforts near U.S. corporate headquarters, tucked safely away from the prying eyes of potential imitators. However, as foreign companies began developing new technologies abroad, technologies often superior to those developed in the United States, U.S. multinationals, even in oligopolistic industries, began rethinking where best to site certain innovative activities. As in the case of retaliatory action by multinationals encroached upon one another's home markets, the same defensive reaction applies to competitive innovation abroad. When the Japanese and West Germans began targeting innovations for the U.S. market, U.S. multinationals countered by establishing R&D and other entrepreneurial units in those countries.

Another element inhibiting innovation abroad by U.S. multinationals involves institutional factors. These include the tendency to have foreign subsidiaries concentrate on gaining market share or implementing transferred technology rather than developing their own innovations. This trend had the effect of depriving subsidiaries of an integral part of the innovation learning process. Finally, the corporate culture of U.S. firms tended to send tacit signals that innovative activity and decision making would reside in the United States, where the lion's share of entrepreneurial skills also were located, and subsidiary managers were discouraged from challenging the sagacity of U.S. managers.

Finally, innovation abroad by U.S. multinationals differs according to their market orientation (refer to discussion in Chapter 2). Multinationals with a local market orientation tend to respond to competitive threats posed by national firms, but the effects of such competition are less pernicious (and far more subtle) than the effects of competition upon multinationals with a world market orientation. As George Yip suggests, multinationals with a world market orientation also tend to operate as oligopolies.[3] National firms develop niches in various markets, and world-market oriented multinationals tend to recognize that the encroachment of these niches would only further wedge apart the fissures that had developed. Thus, in order to stem the insidious wedging effects of foreign firms into those market niches, which could fragment the market and destabilize the oligopolist structure, U.S. multinationals with a world-market orientation would be more likely to respond with proinnovation strategies.

Bearing all this in mind, the discussion now shifts to how U.S. multinationals might draw upon the experience of U.S. start-up entrepreneurial firms in structuring subsidiaries to innovate abroad.

THE CLASSES AND ORIENTATIONS OF INNOVATING SUBSIDIARIES

Any innovation-oriented business endeavor, whether a small start-up entrepreneurial firm or the foreign subsidiary of a large U.S. multinational, will early in its infancy confront a series of survival-threatening crises. These crises are inevitable by virtue of the fact that all innovating companies are involved with the *new*—new technologies, new products, even new services—and their fields of scope are necessarily focused upon activities and markets in which uncertainty reigns supreme. Cast into waters of treacherous tides and invisible undertows, they will sink or swim depending upon how masterfully and swiftly they respond to these crises and uncertainties. This is a guiding premise of this book, and one in which the proactive innovator must never lose sight.

Entrepreneurial units of foreign subsidiaries of U.S. multinationals fall into one of three basis classes—technology monopoly, product, and service—which in turn relate to one of three approaches to innovation—team, dual (a mix of technology monopoly and service), and financial. Into which of the latter orientations a subsidiary will fall is determined in part by the particular stage of a subsidiary's technology monopoly (discussed in depth in Chapter 2).

Crisis response among innovating subsidiaries crucially concerns how managers deal with external and internal crises. Large, traditional, noninnovating corporations have grown and matured such that their activities and financial flows have become essentially routinized and predictable; they do not encounter crises to the severity and frequency experienced by innovating subsidiaries, and may be said to have reached a state of "corporate equilibrium." However, subsidiaries innovating in foreign markets, because they operate under conditions of extreme uncertainty, experience one potentially debilitating crisis after another. Each crisis forces them to shift focus upon external and internal resources, with sometimes dizzying effect.

Internal resources are those resources indigenous to and carried out within the confines of the subsidiary itself. An in-house R&D laboratory, a self-contained manufacturing facility, a strong and effective marketing department—these are all examples of internal resources. External resources, on the other hand, are those drawn from outside the subsidiary. Examples include start-up and initial operating capital (almost always provided by the parent company), contracted-for legal services, consultants hired to analyze host-country demand and market characteristics, independent advertising agencies, and so forth.

As a general rule, when first innovating for a market abroad, the subsidiary is driven by virtue of inexperience and various uncertainties to draw more heavily upon external than internal resources. For example, a subsidiary geared more toward incremental than breakthrough innovations will rely, at least initially, more heavily upon technical support transferred to it directly from the corporate parent. However, as it successfully weathers crisis after crisis, and progressively renders through experience certain uncertainties increasingly impotent, the subsidiary will find itself internalizing many once-external resources. For example, as it begins earning profits through actual marketing of its product, the subsidiary gradually will use these profits to sustain its own operations, thus slowly obviating the need for external sources of funds. Or as it successfully markets its product, the activities of fine-tuning it in response to specific demand characteristics or market niches may be shifted in-house, and the subsidiary's reliance on incremental innovations transferred from its parent will decline accordingly. Or as it gains in actual operating experience and uncertainties decline, the subsidiary may shed reliance upon host-country marketing consultants in favor of establishing and integrating a formal marketing department within its own organizational structure.

When a subsidiary evaluates whether or not to internalize a once-external resource, it must of course take into consideration certain cost/benefit trade-offs. The internalization of some resources (such as establishing an in-house legal department, say) sometimes entails substantial overhead costs. If such action is undertaken prematurely, and the new legal department finds itself subjected to long periods of slack activity, the subsidiary may discover *post facto* that it would have been more cost- and management-effective to have continued drawing upon external resources on an as-need basis, rather than bearing the expenses of this unused internal capacity. Or it may find that some amalgamation of the two approaches might be the wisest course.

An example illustrates. In the early 1980s, several Western European subsidiaries of Dow Chemical Company developed a specialty herbicide, Lontrel™, for control of problem weeds that were endemic to small grains in that market. Dow's Western European subsidiaries developed and later marketed the product themselves, but Dow initially decided that it was more cost-effective to license the manufacture of Lontrel™ to an unaffiliated, independent European firm. Part of the rationale for this approach involved Dow's decision to shift the costs of developing the manufacturing process steps and economies-of-scale to the independent contractor; the arrangement further allowed Dow to take advantage of certain host-country tax structures. The licensing agreement was constructed in such a way as to ensure that the technology remained proprietary to Dow. The product now accounts for over $50 million in sales to the European market and another $50 million in other global markets, including the United States.[4]

Particularly for an innovating subsidiary in its early stages, such decisions about how to balance internal and external resources may prove key to survival. In most cases, how to do so will be determined by the specific exigencies of each individual crisis. For example, an unforeseen shift in host-country political policies may suddenly alter import/export tariff structures in such a way that the subsidiary may find it financially wiser to purchase raw materials from a host-country importer rather than from companies based overseas. In such event, the subsidiary, in order to restructure purchasing contracts, may suddenly find a need to hire legal advisers familiar with the new laws. Other examples of how crises force a reapportioning between internal and external resources are bountiful.

Other influences are associated with the various stages an innovation is in. For instance, when a subsidiary first undertakes the development of an innovation, R&D activities will receive financial priority; however, when the R&D department has successfully designed and developed the innovation, financial priority might shift to manufacturing efforts, and the R&D department—now in a slack period—might shift its attention more to marketing, advertising, or other commercialization-supportive objectives (or the R&D department might refocus its energies upon developing another new technology).

Whatever the case, as the subsidiary gains in actual operating experience, the intensity and frequency of these realignments should become less and less severe. Eventually it will reach a state of equilibrium wherein a balance between internal and external resources has become basically constant, and future plans can be accurately formulated based upon that equilibrium.

Each of the three classes of subsidiaries—technology monopoly, product, and service—operates under fundamentally different conditions and thus may face different sets of crises. This in turn affects how best each might manage internal and external resources. To this issue we now turn.

Types of Subsidiaries

The subsidiaries of U.S. multinationals fall into one of three classes: technology monopoly, product, or service. A subsidiary with a technology monopoly orientation basically is concerned with developing a radical or breakthrough innovation that shows promise of founding a technology monopoly. The product-oriented subsidiary works with an already-established product and focuses attention upon incremental improvements to it, concurrent with pursuing a service-oriented approach in marketing that product. And the service-oriented subsidiary, examples of which range from software companies to firms that specialize in acidizing wells, works to apply mature technologies and emphasizes efforts to bolster market share through marketing/advertising activities, assurance of customer satisfaction, reliance on brand name loyalty, uniqueness of service provided, and so forth. The impact of technology monopoly declines through each of the three successive stages.

The borders among these three classes are rarely so clear-cut, however. Just as the product class draws from elements of the other two, so might the subsidiary whose efforts are focused on developing a technology monopoly pull in service-related characteristics. Thus, a subsidiary developing a fungicide for a particular strain of Bordeaux grape might, as the product approached fruition, explore the potential size of its market (if it had not already done so), or begin the process of establishing efficient product distribution channels and supporting "educational" programs for vinedressers. Likewise, a service-oriented subsidiary, say a long-distance telephone company, might employ innovative fiber optics technology to enhance such service-related factors as audible clarity and lower prices. Thus, the distinctions among these three classes are by no means absolute.

A second caveat is in order here. When a U.S. multinational introduces an innovation abroad, its subsidiary might also offer customer support services, as in the fungicide example above, but a wiser course might be to keep the two functions as separate as possible, by establishing two intercommunicating, but essentially autonomous, subsidiaries. In this instance, resource management issues would tend to be well-defined in each entity, and confusion held to a minimum. Of course, this latter approach will be dictated by the nature of the specific technology, product, and/or service involved; it would not be possible in the fiber optics example but would be for a subsidiary fracting wells in the North Sea that also offered well-maintenance services.

Breakthrough-oriented endeavors are the most likely to produce a technological monopoly, which a multinational subsidiary would then use as its primary advantage over competitors in a given foreign market. At the opposite end of the spectrum, service-oriented subsidiaries tend to deal with products whose technology is mature and hence well-diffused; therefore, its strategic focus is oriented toward the capture of specific, well-defined market niches and assuring consumer satisfaction.

Product firms, however, must develop strategies that incorporate aspects of the other two classes. Because their technologies are maturing and competitors have begun duplicating them, product-oriented firms must distinguish themselves through service characteristics. They are neither oriented exclusively towards technology nor service. They occupy the middle ground, wherein certain challenges lie. For example, management must obey the exigencies of both technology monopoly and service approaches, a dual orientation difficult for managers experienced with one or the other approach but not both. This problem is exacerbated because, as a subsidiary's technology monopoly weakens and its service orientation grows, it must make the transition from one to the other smoothly and well. Failure to do so may well result in the deterioration of competitive advantage at one end, and failure to capture it at the other. If a subsidiary undervalues the positional advantage of its technological monopoly and prematurely turns to a service orientation, it may abort the present advantages of its monopolistic position. Competitors could move quickly to fill the resulting gap and gain both market share and technological expertise at the expense of the subsidiary's misjudgment. Thus, product-oriented companies walk a more precarious tightrope than their cousins.

Three Strategic Approaches to Innovation

Related to these three classes of subsidiaries are three strategic approaches to innovation. This second set was originally developed by venture capitalists as a tool to help them valuate start-up entrepreneurial firms in the United States. Here that tool is extended and applied to innovating subsidiaries abroad.

The three approaches, with their parallels from the first set given in parentheses, are as follows: team (technology monopoly), dual (product), and financial (service). Each is discussed below.

The Team Approach. The team approach is most frequently chosen as the means through which to develop radical or "breakthrough" innovations (as opposed to those achieved by, say, incremental improvements to existing products). A team of scientists, technicians, engineers, and other professionals, perhaps representing a wide variety of fields, is assembled to develop a new product or technology, many of whose specific key characteristics are unknown. An AIDS vaccine is one good example. For the most part, the team approach involves achieving significant breakthroughs that yield a technology monopoly. If a number of teams are racing to develop a given technology first, *time* becomes a critical factor: The winner takes all, in the sense that it seizes propriety ownership of the innovated technology.

Team-oriented endeavors usually are premised on several basic facts about the eventual market for its technology or product. First, there is the perception that future demand will be sufficient to justify the expenses of engaging in a race to be the first to develop an innovation. That is, the innovation usually is seen to have some present practical application; of course, the precise parameters of that future demand are unknown.

Second, the end goal must be perceived as achievable. Basic (or "pure") research is already in-hand; the goal is to convert that basic research into a concrete technology or product. This is a necessary precondition because the expenses of conducting basic or pure research may be out-and-out prohibitive, although research of a less fundamental nature usually will be necessary.

The decision to undertake a team orientation approach also involves cost considerations. The team approach can be expensive. The best available scientists and technologists must be assembled and paid, support staff brought together, and state-of-the-art R&D laboratories equipped and set in place. The cost of assembling the team and seeing its efforts underway may be viewed as the *minimum* or base cost, against which the eventual value of the technology or product to be innovated must be measured. For example, the cost-worthiness of assembling a team to find a substitute for penicillin would be balanced against the extent to which penicillin has saturated the market for antibiotics.

This cost/benefit approach can become quite complex. For instance, particularly in oligopolies when similar firms are competing to develop a similar product, valuation may crucially turn upon the cost of a foregone opportunity. In the aluminum industry, ceramics is now viewed as being a possible future substitute for some applications of aluminum. Thus, the value to Alcoa of investing in a fledgling ceramics research team may be trivial compared to the profits lost if it fails to develop or pursue certain ceramics technologies itself. Further, even if failing to be the first to achieve the breakthrough, Alcoa might find the basic research conducted by its team invaluable when entering the ceramics-substitution market; that is, it need not play "catch-up" at some subsequent stage.

The team approach is less risky than the dual approach but more risky than the financial approach. First, the rewards of developing a technology monopoly may be handsome indeed. Second, even if the team fails, the basic research it has conducted may yield peripheral products or ideas that can be put to profitable use in a different context. Third, even if a team "loses" the race to develop an innovation, it still will have taken giant strides in gaining knowledge about that innovation, knowledge that may give it an edge over other, more laggardly competitors. One example might be when the "loser" team uses the experience and expertise gained in trying to develop a particular innovation in adapting it for commercialization in a particular market segment the lead innovator has not captured.

Fourth, even if failing to "win" to race to innovate, the subsidiary may still salvage a portion of its initial investment through the sale or licensing of patents or other proprietary information or processes developed during the R&D effort. In other words, in the team approach all capital is not necessarily sunk; there are a variety of ways either to retrieve a portion of that capital or to reapply certain side-benefits of the team approach.

There is a somewhat complex, fifth aspect. Sometimes, when the team approach results in the *successful* development of an innovation, particularly one having very wide market demand, the basis of an oligopoly begins. As competitors enter and the oligopoly forms, the oligopoly helps member firms to realize profits higher than would be possible in a purely competitive market in which price equals marginal cost.

The Dual Approach. The dual (technological/service) approach (which corresponds with the product orientation) is best suited for that stage in which markets are well-defined, product characteristics known, and technology monopolies partially or well diffused. This approach relies on incremental improvements to existing technology rather than on breakthrough innovations (although incremental improvements have been known to yield breakthrough innovations) concurrent with a service orientation. That is, the subsidiary focuses a portion of its activity on identifying new market niches (or on recasting or solidifying existing markets) or service-oriented opportunities and gears product development accordingly.

The dual approach is the most risky of the three. Although it relies upon an existing, proven technology, success depends crucially upon the market responses. Whether a subsidiary can consolidate a fragmented market or whether its product will attract buyers sufficient to justify production remains unknown until commercialization is actually underway. And the process of bringing a product to commercialization involves considerable expense, particularly at the manufacturing end.

Vital to the success of the dual approach is research: not just into technological matters, which are decreasingly important, but rather research to gauge consumer demand, to identify existing and potential market trends, and to otherwise reduce uncertainties. Assuming this research is successful, the next step is to take that knowledge and apply it to production and financial exigencies. All three functions must be smoothly and comprehensively integrated to serve the subsidiary's commercial goals; and the failure of any one component to interact with the others may signal the collapse of the enterprise as a whole. Thus, this approach requires a high degree of structural fluidity among the subsidiary's various departments.

In some cases, the dual approach may act to redefine an existing market in ways that make it unique; that is, it may apply an existing technology or product to carve out an entirely new market niche in an otherwise stable, well-established market. The dual approach sometimes entails significant chunks of sunk capital; money spent on advertising, for example, is essentially irretrievable if the venture fails. The vast sums spent to construct, equip, and staff a manufacturing facility are also largely unsalvageable, a significant factor particularly when a competitor's breakthrough innovation suddenly and radically alters demand for the subsidiary's product. Likewise, dual-oriented subsidiaries are highly vulnerable to abrupt shifts in the supply and prices of such core factors of production as energy (disruptions in natural gas supply, oil price hikes), labor (strikes), and so forth. Host-country political actions, which might range from nationalization of foreign-owned industries to abrupt changes in tax laws, also contribute to the riskiness of this approach.

In short, the dual approach is the most complex of the three, and managing the variety of influences and uncertainties to which it is subject requires a highly adaptable and keenly sensitive management. Management must be capable of first seeing, then seizing upon market opportunities as they arise; this is much less true for the team approach, where management's concerns are less focused upon the particularities and foibles of a largely unknown market. Further, although the dual approach may successfully identify a small market niche for its product, unless there is substantial potential that that niche will grow, the endeavor may prove unprofitable in the longer term.

Even though research may fail to identify fruitful market niches, it nonetheless may yield valuable side-benefits. Research may help to eliminate inappropriate markets, identify trends that are *not* developing, or otherwise produce contradictory evidence. At one extreme, such research may terminate the endeavor flat in its tracks, but more commonly it will help mangement to focus the subsidiary's resources and product development efforts to better advantage.

In addition to technological and service components, the success of the dual approach is also dependent upon a host of other disparate factors. A keen, finely-targeted advertising strategy may be crucial, particularly absent brand-name loyalty, as also might be establishing efficient channels of distribution, supply of raw materials, the competency of staff, and so forth.

The Financial Approach. The financial approach (which correlates directly with the service orientation) most commonly appears among subsidiaries that are established, well-functioning, reliant upon a mature technology, and customer-service-oriented. Unlike the technology monopoly or dual-oriented subsidiaries, the financially-oriented subsidiary has well-established cash flows, operates in a well-known market, and enjoys predictability of demand for the service(s) it offers. Innovations, if any, tend to congregate around procedural efficiencies, such as improvements to manufacturing economies-of-scale, leveraged buy-outs of sagging competitors, improvement in support industries, and so forth.

The level of risk is lowest for the financial approach. Past and present cash flows yield stable empirical information upon which to forecast future expenses and profits; uncertainty is low. Further, because financially-oriented subsidiaries are less subject to the sudden crises and traumatic disruptions experienced by the other two approaches, they enjoy a degree of security unknown to the others. For the most part, these subsidiaries are fairly mature, and stable. Many enjoy the benefits of well-established reputations or brand-name loyalty, and thus hefty expenditures for basic R&D or market research are unnecessary.

Costs tend to be stable in financially-oriented subsidiaries, which belong to maturing industries. A team-oriented subsidiary may suddenly be confronted with an immediate need to increase R&D expenditures three or four times above that projected; likewise, a dual-oriented subsidiary may find that it must triple or quadruple advertising, promotion, and/or distribution costs due to unforeseen circumstances. But in financially-oriented subsidiaries, the costs of manufacturing, personnel, advertising, and so forth are both stable and predictable. Further, the need for future substantial capital investment is minimal, as such subsidiaries tend to rely more on maintenance of existing capital equipment rather than on purchase and installation of new equipment. Thus, managers in financially-oriented subsidiaries tend to focus efforts on cost reductions through efficiency gains, a sensible approach particularly in industries that tend to experience only slow, incremental growth.

A final consideration is that most service-oriented subsidiaries belong to either extremely concentrated or extremely fragmented industries. In concentrated industries, a handful of major firms have a firm lock on a significant portion of market share, and less efficient firms have been forced out of the market. A subsidiary in such a position is unlikely to rock the boat by undertaking innovative activities; concentrated industries also discourage start-up entrants. On the other hand, in fragmented industries, the industry as a whole usually has not achieved the economies of scale that would allow for rationalization that leads to concentration as a result of breakthrough, brand-name loyalty, or high capital investments.

SUMMARY

This chapter has divided innovative subsidies into three generic classes, each of which relates to a specific strategic approach and each of which must manage internal/external resources in ways determined by the specific crises each encounters. The maturation of technological monopolies is shown to be a crucial parameter in determining into which class an innovative subsidiary will fall. It should be pointed out that all these considerations are in a continual state of flux; that is, a subsidiary will tend over time to move from a more technology-monopoly to a more service orientation, unless either radical or incremental innovations are introduced to maintain that subsidiary's current orientation.

NOTES

1. Author's interview with the manager of a U.S. multinational, proprietary.

2. James Brian Quinn, "Technology Transfer by Multinational Companies," in *Harvard Business Review,* November/December 1969, reprint.

3. George Yip, interview.

4. Author's interview with Dow Chemical Company manager, proprietary.

PART II

The foregoing chapters have examined a number of general conditions and factors shaping U.S. multinational activities in foreign markets over the past four decades. In their early heyday of virtually undisputed sovereignty in foreign markets, U.S. multinationals directly exported innovations developed for U.S. consumers for sale overseas, making adjustments in product design as needed and enjoying a range of technological monopolies that initially were not subject to threats from competitors. In time, however, all technological monopolies become diffused to competitors and this fact, along with certain other developments, gradually lowered the barriers to entry of other competitors. Both non–U.S. multinationals (most prominently Japanese and West German) and national (local) firms then began competing head-on with U.S. multinationals in markets abroad, and more recently in U.S. domestic markets as well. The U.S. multinational reaction to competitive threat, as we have seen, historically has been defensive in nature; that is, where such threat arose, U.S. multinationals responded by establishing first manufacturing, then R&D facilities, abroad, at the same time increasing the rate of technology transfers to their foreign subsidiaries.

However, competitors then introduced a crucial twist: they began targeting innovations *specifically* for markets abroad. In light of this new tactic, the old, defensive strategy of some U.S. multinationals became inadequate, and as that proved out, some began to rethink their existing, defensive strategy, turning to innovation abroad and using as springboards manufacturing and R&D facilities already sited in foreign countries, as well as other supportive advantages. Part I of this text devoted the bulk of its discussion to analyzing the factors that helped U.S. multinationals to innovate abroad successfully.

Thus, Part I has laid the groundwork with which U.S. multinationals might assess whether, and to what degree, they already have in place the necessary instruments and conditions with which they might more proactively innovate abroad. The most basic is the presence of *motivation*. A U.S. multinational historically has been more likely to be motivated the more it has at stake; that is, the greater its share of profits from sales abroad and the greater the competitive threat to those sales, the more likely it will innovate as a defensive measure.

The likelihood of success is measured by a range of other factors. These include length of experience operating abroad, commitment to R&D, the sources of competitive threats in overseas markets, and so forth.

At this juncture the discussion takes a leap forward. Part I examined *past* U.S. multinational experiences in markets abroad, but recapturing or creating new foreign markets in many cases now will require a *proactive* strategy. And although the roots of a successful proactive strategy still depend in great measure upon those same factors that make a defensive response successful, additional elements also must come into play. Some of these elements were touched upon throughout Part I; here they are drawn together and focused into two areas of discussion: control systems and managers.

The shift to a proactive strategy shares at least one fundamental characteristic with the defensive strategy: the importance of overcoming uncertainty. Part I outlined several mechanisms that U.S. multinationals have found to be useful in reducing such uncertainty, but undertaking a proactive strategy, which is inherently a more offensively-oriented and hence a much riskier endeavor, requires concomitantly bolder measures. One such mechanism, found to be highly useful in small U.S. start-up entrepreneurial firms, is the establishment of a "custom-designed" control system; that is, a control system designed specifically for an entrepreneurial business activity. Such control systems are constructed so as to integrate the various functions of the subsidiary in such a way that they all serve the same end goal—to produce an innovation (or to bring it to market)—at the same time they encourage structural flexibility that uses information and knowledge gained from crises in ways that reduce uncertainty. The control system, as discussed in Chapter 5, thus becomes a feedstock mechanism that provides crucial information for planning, budgeting, performance measurement, and incentive systems. Although the basic structure of the subsidiary remains essentially the same, the control system is used as a dynamic tool with which management shifts emphasis among elements in response to what it learns from crises.

However, a control system is at its heart only a tool to be used by management, and any innovative enterprise, but particularly those oriented toward foreign markets, requires managers who have special talents and characteristics. Chapters 6 and 7 tackle this subject accordingly, focusing upon "organizational entrepreneurs"—those managers who work within the parent and/or subsidiary organizational structure to originate an innovative idea and/or work to follow it through to commercial fruition. Chapter 7 concludes with a brief discussion of several specific steps managers can take to help ensure the success of pursuing a proactive strategy for innovating abroad.

The stakes are not trivial. Are Japanese automotive companies to continue establishing manufacturing plants here in the United States, using U.S. workers to produce cars for U.S. consumers, with profits flowing back to Japan? Are U.S. multinationals to continue facing the gradual erosion of their overseas market shares, as pursuit of the old, defensive responses to competition forces them to play the role of second-best or "catch-up"? Finally, does it really *cost* that much to undertake a proactive strategy? The following chapters address these questions and find that the necessary changes are more psychological than structural, more adaptive than disruptive, more feet-on-the-ground than pie-in-the-sky. A reorientation by U.S. multinationals from a defensive to a proactive strategy could very well make a crucial difference in the future health of U.S. multinationals, and a great deal more than national pride rests in the balance.

Control Systems for Innovation Abroad

In traditional corporations, control systems are umbrella mechanisms constructed to evaluate how well the corporation is faring in achieving its desired goals, where in various departments improvements can be made, and how interaction among those various departments can better serve those goals. Some control systems are micro in focus—designed to better achieve economies of scale in a given manufacturing process, say—and others are more macro—how to mesh various activities more effectively. In any event, they are a tool, an instrument that *management* uses. Control systems are, in a sense, a *proxy* for managerial effectiveness, in that a good control system poorly used can never rise above the competence of its management. And the subsidiaries of U.S. multinationals that are proactively innovating abroad, because they face such a high degree of uncertainty in their endeavors, have an even greater need to institute control systems, but ones designed along nontraditional lines. The activities of a corporation (or subsidiary) may be divided into four basic functions: R&D, financing/budgeting, manufacturing/production, and marketing/sales. The control systems with which we are concerned here, those for innovating subsidiaries abroad, thus oversee how these four structural elements interact and change in response to uncertainty, to crises, to opportunities.

Control systems designed for innovative subsidiaries abroad (and for small start-up entrepreneurial firms here in the United States) are considerably more dynamic and far-reaching than those designed for traditional companies. In innovation-oriented firms, control systems act to oversee the intimate, rapid, and effective interaction of the four functions listed above. However, it should be pointed out that rarely if ever is the establishment of a control system an *immediate* priority when first undertaking an innovative endeavor, for the perfectly understandable reason that only until all four basic functions are in place and operating reasonably well will there be anything to control.

This chapter draws upon research conducted by the author into 50 entrepreneurial start-up firms in the United States and extends and modifies that research to U.S. multinational subsidiaries innovating abroad. The methodology of that survey is discussed at length, and then the chapter proceeds to compare traditional versus nontraditional (that is, innovation-oriented) firms in terms of how their control systems address crises and uncertainties and how resource constraints are affected. The focus then shifts to a discussion of control systems designed specifically for innovating subsidiaries, with specific attention to how such control systems can better serve the planning, budgeting, performance measurement, and incentive system functions.

SURVEY OF FIFTY U.S. START-UP ENTREPRENEURIAL FIRMS

The analysis of this chapter is based in part on the author's survey of fifty start-up entrepreneurial firms in the United States. This section summarizes that survey prior to applying its findings to U.S. multinational subsidiaries innovating abroad.

The survey does not claim to be statistically representative; rather, data and results gleaned from interviews are used for illustrative purposes only. The sample population encompassed both successful and unsuccessful start-up firms, the measure of success being whether a firm was still an on-going concern three years after the date of the first infusion of capital.

The survey reflects several important biases. First, the sample base derived largely from information furnished by venture capitalists who provide capital for start-up firms. Investors, of course, commit resources only after having favorably assessed the prospects of a firm's future growth and profitability; it therefore follows that, at the time of capital infusion, these firms had progressed from being solely R&D- or concept-oriented to inchoative commercial enterprises. Second, the firms are likely to have registered few, if any, actual sales. Third, control systems for these firms necessarily would appear only *after* capital infusion, for reasons given above. And fourth, interviews with managers found that in some cases venture capitalists *required* firms to implement control systems, as a means of protecting their investments. A broader sample base might significantly obviate these biases; in addition, it would likely reveal a wider range in the timing of control system implementation.

The sample selected only start-up entrepreneurial firms that were self-contained (i.e., independently organized) and whose efforts were generally directed toward a single, well-defined, overall goal. (Although five start-up firms *were* linked to corporate parents, all five functioned largely independently, with boards of directors and top managers not directly beholden to the parent; that is, they functioned more or less autonomously. Thus, they are included with the self-contained firms.)

The survey excluded those entrepreneurial start-up firms if the actions of their corporate parents were seen as potentially influencing their establishment and operation. One criterion of exclusion was the poor partitioning of the entrepreneurial activities of the start-up from the routine business of the corporate parent; for example, a firm would be excluded if one or more of its key managers held dual responsibilities in both arenas (child and parent). The rationale for this is based on the presumption that such dual-role managers might exert undue influence on the start-up firm, because those managers might be pressured by parent-imposed incentive and performance criteria to shape the start-up's control system in one way or another. The second criterion of exclusion involved the nonsegmentation of the start-up and parent firms into different subunits.

The cutoff point for establishing control systems was chosen to be three months after first capital infusion. This standard reflects a consensus by both venture capitalists and managers of entrepreneurial firms. Several observations on this subject are in order here. First, by necessity, most start-up firms will defer establishing a control system until the essential activities of the firm are underway. Or delay may reflect other difficulties endemic to start-up firms, such as slowness in surmounting certain initial financial, technological, or marketing barriers. As the survey could not account for these effects, this *caveat* should be borne in mind.

The data provide the basis for another observation regarding the timing of control system implementation. Of the ten successful start-up firms that had *not* implemented control systems within three months after capital infusion, seven did so within twelve months, and the remaining three within twenty-four months. Interviews with managers from all ten firms found that the motivation for eventually instituting a control system arose in response to a *crisis*—usually financial and usually one that threatened to provoke serious cost overruns.

Of the seven firms that were less slow to implement, managers stated that control systems played a strong, albeit not critical role, in their firms' success. Of the three firms that were slowest to implement control systems, it is debatable whether their eventual introduction played a crucial role in success; interviews suggested that these firms were already successful.

Additionally, we selected the point of capital infusion as a proxy for the organizational and financial scales that could utilize an entrepreneurial control system. The survey data confirm the appropriateness of the methodology. Firms in the sample used "seed" financing or the personal equity of entrepreneurs in developing a business plan and exploring its feasibility (through, say, market studies, research into the ease and viability of relevant product technology improvements, and so forth). In almost all instances, the firms had yet to begin sales. It was not until just *after* capital infusion that these start-up firms had the organizational and financial scope that merited establishment of an individualized control system.

The procedure used to determine whether a firm had instituted an entrepreneurial (as opposed to conventional) control system involved a simple, two-part test. First, the presence of an independent accounting/bookkeeping system disqualified that firm from consideration; all fifty firms had integrated their accounting/bookkeeping functions with other primary functions. Second, within three months of capital infusion, the firm had to be engaged in four generic, interrelated activities: planning, budgeting, performance measurement, and incentive systems.

The interrelationships among the four activities above will differ from firm to firm. Some may emphasize the link between budgeting and performance measures; others may emphasize the link between budgeting and the incentive system, all to varying degrees of intensity.

One further refinement should be noted. When an innovative firm is establishing a control system—data show that many do not—it must be explicitly molded to be responsive to current needs and strategies of the start-up firm. Thus, the process of developing (or later adapting) a start-up firm's control system entails establishing objectives, and goals that, like marketing or manufacturing, are complementary to the overall strategy.

Methodology

Survey results support the hypothesis that establishing a flexible entrepreneurial control system correlates positively with success (see Table 5.1). Firms that either delayed establishing control systems or equated them with only the accounting/bookkeeping function were demonstrably less successful.

Data fall into four categories: success/failure correlated with the presence/absence of an entrepreneurial control system. Of the fifty firms, which include both those with and without control systems, twenty-nine (58 percent) were ranked as successful, and twenty-one (42 percent) were not. Twenty-eight (56 percent) established control systems; twenty-two did not. Of the twenty-eight firms that did *not* have control systems, only ten (45 percent) were successful. All else being equal, this suggests that the implementation of an entrepreneurial control system enhances the chances of success by about 50 percent ($0.68 \div 0.45$).

Even if success occurred randomly 58 percent of the time,

Table 5.1
Correlation between Successful Start-up Firms and Control
Systems

	Successful Firms	Unsuccessful Firms	Total
Entrepreneurial control systems	19	9	28
Lack of entrepreneurial control systems	10	12	22
Totals	29	21	50

Source: Author's survey of 50 start-up entrepreneurial firms

and 56 percent of the firms still implemented entrepreneurial control systems, a simple joint-probability analysis shows that 32 percent (0.58 × 0.56) of the firms still would be expected to succeed (see Table 5.2). In fact, data show that 38 percent did succeed. Of the successful firms without influence by the control systems, the expectation is that 55 percent would develop control systems (0.32 ÷ 0.58). In fact, data show that 65 percent of the successful firms did install control systems. This simple data analysis thus further supports a positive correlation between establishment of control systems and success.

Table 5.2
Comparison of Data with Joint Probabilities

	Successful Firms	Unsuccessful Firms	Total
Entrepreneurial control systems	.38* .32	.18 .24	.56
Lack of entrepreneurial control systems	.20 .26	.24 .18	.44
Totals	.58	.42	1.00

Source: Author's survey of 50 start-up entrepreneurial firms

Although data tend to support that positive correlation, by no means is the evidence overwhelming. As Table 5.2 indicates, the presence of a control system correlates with success at a level only slightly higher than random probability (as derived by the joint-probability analysis above). This proximity of actual to random would be worrisome, were it not for the presence of other factors.

For instance, entrepreneurial control systems cannot counteract the crippling or potentially fatal results of a precipitous technological failure, grossly inaccurate or inept marketing programs, or preemption of market share by competitors. Under such circumstances, the presence of control systems would not be able to salvage the enterprise.

Another possible influence is management. Managers experienced in innovative endeavors tend to recognize the benefits of establishing entrepreneurial control systems; to them, it may be equal in importance to such other essential activities as product development and implementation of marketing strategies. Thus, in some instances, the presence of control systems in fact may reflect managerial adroitness.

CONTROL SYSTEMS AND INNOVATIVE SUBSIDIARIES ABROAD

In extending the survey results to innovating subsidiaries abroad, a handy frame of reference is to compare some characteristics of innovative subsidiaries with those of conventional noninnovating firms. There are two fundamental differences.

First, an innovative subsidiary confronts a host of critical uncertainties that impact on all four of its basic functions, uncertainties that traditional noninnovating firms do not experience to such a daunting degree. In part due to these uncertainties, the innovating subsidiary early in its existence will inevitably confront a series of survival-threatening problems or crises, both internal and external to the company. Responding quickly and effectively to these crises frequently entails instituting short-term solutions (a thumb-in-the-dam scenario), but of these short-term solutions many involve a near-instantaneous realignment of the subsidiary's priorities and strategies; all other activities must be dropped to focus on the immediate problem.

The second major characteristic of innovating subsidiaries relates to resource constraints. Start-up firms in the United States tend to experience these more as financial constraints, and overseas subsidiaries, more as managerial. To give an example: A start-up U.S. entrepreneurial firm developing, say, laser equipment for a new cataract surgical procedure may find the sudden need to develop a prototype model. To construct such a machine would require the infusion of new capital. On the other hand, an innovation-oriented subsidiary would tend more to enjoy access to a pool of capital available through its parent multinational.

Because it continually must rely on the expertise of persons familiar with conditions specific to the host-country, however, the subsidiary may at different stages require different forms of dexterity from its managers. That is, as crises arise and priorities change, management must shift resources in ways that are highly adaptable. There is no room for rigidity. Hence, control systems developed for innovating subsidiaries are more oriented toward a managerial cast; those for entrepreneurial start-up firms have more of a financial cast.

Traditional firms adhere to conventional, well-trod paths in achieving their goals. But innovation-oriented subsidiaries have no such well-trod paths to follow. Traditional firms weigh their progress and evaluate the success of their strategies according to whether concrete and relatively short-term objectives have been met. But for an innovation-oriented subsidiary, such measures may prove, particularly in times of crisis, to be straw dogs. How can success be measured in terms of sales as an indication of the subsidiary's inroads into market share when the market is essentially unknown to it? Instead, these subsidiaries must continually translate subjective judgments (that is, nonquantifiable) into objectively-verifiable measures.

Control systems tailored to a subsidiary's specific needs help buffer against crises in two general ways. First, they provide some forewarning of financial or resource crises. Second, control systems communicate through financial data and performance incentives in ways that motivate managers to work cooperatively in achieving common strategic objectives.

Control systems individually designed for innovating subsidiaries differ in two regards from those designed for traditional corporations. First, those designed for the subsidiary firm must be flexible enough to accommodate frequent realignments of its short-term strategies and priorities. Second, they provide subjective information or "feedback" that managers must translate into concrete, objectively-verifiable measures. For example, a manager whose major subjective goal is to establish market acceptance for a new product may translate that goal into the concrete objective of attaining market share or a specific sales volume within a given time frame. Concrete objectives in traditional firms often—but not necessarily—appear as financial measures, such as profit levels or returns on investment. On the other hand, in innovating subsidiaries, managers define objectives in largely nonfinancial terms, such as achieving market penetration or major technical developments. In many cases, those objectives involve time considerations, in the sense that the more rapidly a technology is developed, the greater are its chances of becoming a market leader (see Chapter 2 for further discussion).

Because it operates under certain resource handicaps, the subsidiary must restrict the scope of its control system to the most effective usage. This constraint has the beneficial side effect of forcing managers to focus only on issues that are immediately essential.

And just as each crisis provokes a different type of strategic response, so must the critical variables change over time and with differing conditions to be consistent with those different types of strategies. For example, in the case of NAVA, an Italian-based firm marketing an innovative ski boot/binding system, critical variables emphasized management's assessment of what elements were essential to achieve market penetration. This subjective decision then led to the establishment of a series of concrete objectives for every phase of the control system. Operating costs were to subsume cost of in-store displays for each dealer; management revised the procedure for allocating discretionary advertising costs and also redefined the center of responsibility for advertising; an aggressive incentive plan was developed to encourage salesmen to contract with new dealerships. All these changes stemmed from management's subjective assessments of strategic implications; all were then translated into objective, measurable goals.

This process of using subjective assessments to develop concrete, measurable objectives requires the creation of somewhat unconventional control systems. For example, the NAVA management established incentives for sales people based not only on the number of systems sold to existing dealers—a conventional approach—but also on the number of *new* dealers signed up as well. Second, rather than being measured strictly as a profit or investment center, the NAVA sales department was measured by the cost per dealer. Both these measurements reflect the subjective judgments of management, judgments that proved critical to the company's long-term success. Conventional control systems of traditional corporations do not take such approaches.

Developing concrete objectives based upon subjective judgments usually involves a process of consensus-building among key managers. For the most part, innovative subsidiaries cannot formulate their planning decisions based on historical data (being new, they have none) or on the actions of competitive firms (they may be irrelevant to the subsidiary's strategy). All they have to formulate strategy with is interpretation of existing market conditions and subjective or intuitive assessments; however, there are advantages to this handicap, because it affords the subsidiary manager great latitude in choosing from a diverse set of interpretations of appropriate strategies.

INNOVATIVE SUBSIDIARIES AND CONTROL SYSTEMS: THE FOUR COMPONENTS

Having established the importance of control systems in innovative subsidiaries abroad, the discussion now turns to how such control systems may influence the subsidiary's four basic functions: planning, budgeting, performance measurements, and incentive systems.

First, it is worth mentioning that some entrepreneurs, particularly those whose major interest lies with the innovative *concept* (as opposed to its commercial execution) find the detailed attention demanded by control systems to be a bothersome distraction from the business of creating. This applies more to entrepreneurs in smaller start-up firms in the United States than to innovating subsidiaries of U.S. multinationals, but parallels exist. Pier Lugi Nava, the impetuous Italian entrepreneur behind the innovative NAVA ski boot/binding system, which has been successfully marketed in European markets and currently is penetrating U.S. markets, speaks for many innovation-oriented entrepreneurs when he says:

I cannot spend valuable time thinking about a control system. It's absolutely contrary to my personality and to what I can best offer the business. What I need to be doing is thinking about new products, new designs, the needs of skiers. Not how I should be restricting the ideas I pioneered. I know control is important; I just don't have the time or patience for it. Control only dampens the imagination, and without my imagination I am useless.[1]

Once the activities of an innovative subsidiary are underway, an effective control system can be designed and set in place. And a successful control system uses four tools in an innovation-oriented subsidiary, tools used in ways very different from control systems designed for traditional firms.

Planning

When developing long-term planning goals, a traditional firm draws and extrapolates from its own past experiences, from those of its competitors, and from historical data to estimate expected costs, production volumes, sales, and other variables critical to planning. It is not so much that such managers are myopic as much as they are conventionally conservative, as presumably they are paid to be. An innovating subsidiary enjoys no such advantage however. Precisely because they are in the vanguard of a particular market segment, technology, or product, they cannot draw upon quantitative, year-in/year-out information when developing their planning goals; they have no base of past operating experience upon which to draw. Instead, they must rely upon *subjective* criteria in making planning decisions, and here the control system plays a vital role. Because innovative subsidiaries evolve and learn through a series of crisis/reaction responses, their managers must analyze the feedback engendered by flexible, responsive control systems and translate it into objective terms, which then are applied to developing planning goals.

It should be acknowledged that this distinction between traditional and innovative firms is by no means absolute, but rather is firm-specific. For example, a biotechnological firm that is considering developing a substitute for penicillin might draw upon the historical performance data of analogous products to help determine market potential: however, even this quantitatively-determined data may yield little that is useful. Past patterns do not necessarily apply to new products; thus, information from analogous product marketing may yield little insight as to the effects of licensing hurdles, distribution problems, public acceptance, and so forth. In such cases, the only reasonable alternative is to rely on subjective judgments.

A more useful ground upon which to distinguish traditional from innovative firms is as follows: Most traditional firms define corporate goals in concrete *financial* terms (such as return on investment, profits, and so forth); however, innovating subsidiaries, which operate under constrained resources, must rely more on *nonfinancial* terms.

The challenge for subsidiary managers is how to reconstitute subjective, qualitative assessments into viable, objective planning goals. For instance, a subsidiary that is marketing a new product may view its primary planning objective in terms of market penetration (nonfinancial) rather than in terms of profit returns (financial). Or a subsidiary that is developing a new technology may value lessening the *time* (nonfinancial) in which it is brought to production, rather than cost reductions in the R&D process (financial). Thus, for an innovating subsidiary, objective goals are derived from subjective assessments, expressed in nonfinancial terms; the immediate next step is to express these objectives in concrete, measurable terms (for example, percent of market share, length of time) that then are fed back into the planning process.

The extent to which nonfinancial terms apply to innovative subsidiaries depends on which of two orientations they have. The first is the "team" orientation (see Chapter 4), which is devoted to developing a new technology or process—the exact specifications and technical feasibility of which are unknown—that faces a potentially unconstrained demand market. A biotechnology firm developing an AIDS vaccine might be an example. Absent historical data, planning objectives cannot usefully be stated in financial terms; instead, control systems designed for team-oriented firms will base planning objectives on objective, well-defined, nonfinancial measures that reflect the subjective judgment of the entire team.

The second type of subsidiary control system is dual- (technology/service) oriented. Financial terms for dual-oriented firms' control systems are only slightly more relevant than for team-oriented firms. If engaged in manufacturing, the former can establish cost or return-on-investment measures based upon the experiences of parallel markets. In any case, nonfinancial terms are more pervasive in team- and dual-oriented firms than in traditional firms.

Although long-range planning is crucial to both traditional firms and innovative subsidiaries, there are important distinctions. "Long-range" for traditional firms usually is measured in terms of years; for innovative-subsidiaries, it may be as long as twelve years or as short as three months.

The focus of entrepreneurial subsidiaries, at least in the early stages, is on ensuring short-term survival. Although they obviously are deeply concerned with estimating long-term business potential, reality dictates that they cannot rely much on the accuracy of those estimates when making planning decisions. Instead, each time it passes through a series of crises, an innovating subsidiary's short-range (and sometimes even long-range) plans and strategies must adapt in response to market realities. To stubbornly force the system to adhere to original planning estimates would lead to a dead stall, or worse. Thus, a subsidiary is like a sailboat in a race, in which each competing skipper recognizes the same unaltering long-term objective (to win), but the tactics he uses to get there fluctuate with the strength and direction of the wind, wave action and tides, and the maneuvers of competing sailboats. None of these variables can be predicted; each skipper must swiftly alter his strategy in inventive, subjective, and flexible ways.

Budgeting

Budgeting procedures play a broader, more dynamic role in innovating subsidiaries than in traditional firms. Although as the subsidiary matures its budgeting process will gradually evolve into more of a control tool, in its initial stages, the budget serves more importantly as an index by which to measure the accuracy of projections, and then, based on that analysis, to undertake testing and other responsive measures to correct any flawed strategic and operating assumptions. For instance, budgeting in subsidiaries helps to prevent organizational and financial entropy, either of which might have seriously adverse consequences; thus, in innovating subsidiaries, budgeting is more of a planning than a control tool.

Resource allocation in any business is a critical function of the planning process. But whereas traditional firms have access to a greater stock of capital and many of their budgeting items are routinized, innovating subsidiaries tend to be both capital- and data-constrained. Thus, formal capital investment decisions are made by eliciting the subjective views of all key managers, with the objective of building a consensus. The resulting valuation criteria tend in subsidiaries to constitute a strategic decision, whereas in traditional firms the process tends to result in the establishment of a hurdle rate or quantitative goal.

This approach offers distinct advantages. For instance, it applies peer pressure on all subsidiary managers to perform well, in addition to supplying motivation for a manager to fulfill the goals (both strategic and budgetary) that he himself established: "one for all, and all for one." However, there are two possible perils to this approach. First, the group may tend to develop budget targets that are easily achievable. Second, managers may strive relentlessly to achieve their self-imposed objectives but at the expense of broader financial and strategic objectives. However, this latter temptation is ameliorated to the extent that all managers recognize the common benefits of controlling costs and maintaining quality products and services.

In response to disruptions in operations caused by unforeseeable external influences, innovative subsidiaries might find themselves modifying and revising their budgets on an as-needed basis. This process not only serves to signal trouble spots but it also serves as a feedback mechanism for performance and strategy improvements. Thus, managers of innovating subsidiaries, rather than holding to a static view of variances as being either on or off budget, consider the *dynamics* underlying those variances in determining how to improve monitoring and how to redefine strategy.

In fact, subsidiary managers, if overemphasizing budgetary performance may obscure other critical (and potentially costly) problems. For instance, emphasizing budget requirements at the expense of quality or product improvements would backfire in both the short- and longer-terms and in both financial and nonfinancial terms. In sum, budgeting for an innovating subsidiary is a tool with which to analyze variances in order to better understand and respond to the driving, dynamic economics of the firm; it is not used to control or circumscribe activity, but rather to drive and motivate changes in how resources are allocated.

There is another advantage of having a flexible budgeting process. For instance, if a manager found a significant variance in his share of the budget that he knew was unrelated to his performance, this would indicate the presence of a problem elsewhere. For example, the R&D department might develop a prototype innovation under budget; however, when mass-production begins, due to a design incompatible with the manufacturing system, the budgetary variable may show up on the manufacturing side—although the origin of the problem lay in the faulty R&D design. Likewise, if the marketing department were to discover that successfully selling a product required its diversification, the manufacturing department, having already tooled-up for mass production, would suffer the full weight of the differential. Analyses of such variances thus may provide evidence of a problem located someplace other than where it was initially presumed to lie.

Performance Measures

As with budgeting, performance measurements tend to be dynamic in innovative subsidiaries, and static in large, traditional corporations. In subsidiaries, evidence such as lower costs, increased sales, and successful development of new products tends to accumulate over several periods of time before true performance effectiveness can be discerned. Thus, measures should be flexibly based to account for a length of time; in traditional firms, they are based on a static, single-period measurement. Further, because innovative subsidiaries must translate subjective assessments into concrete, objective goals and strategies, performance measures tend to be based more on nonfinancial criteria, such as increasing market share and achieving technical advances.

Further, in an innovative subsidiary, the performance of a department is evaluated *relative to the strategy* prevailing at that period of time. This is a reasonable approach because if the control system is continually being modified to meet changing conditions, a department's performance may appear to fluctuate widely—unless the effects of strategic changes are factored out. For example, if a department showed significant variance in performance from that expected, but if analysis of the external causes behind that variance identified the improvidence of a certain strategy as being responsible—not the department's ineptitude—then performance might be reassessed favorably. Likewise, the fulfillment of objective measurements that are based on subjective assessments allows innovating subsidiaries to measure performance in relation to the articulated needs and strategies of the firm. Unlike a traditional firm, the innovating subsidiary attaches very little importance to meeting budget projections on a monthly, quarterly, or even annual basis, especially when costs and other objective performance criteria cannot be determined from historical data.

Incentive Systems

How control systems use incentive systems to motivate managers varies greatly between innovating subsidiaries and traditional firms. Many traditional firms apply a fixed formula based on sales volume, market share, and/or profit levels; flexibility in this formula is rare. On the other hand, subsidiaries in their early stages tend to rely on more subjectively-based incentive schemes (based on the perceived efforts of the evaluee), although often also incorporating aspects of the fixed formula approach. Such incentive systems are based on both financial and nonfinancial criteria. As the subsidiary matures, it tends to evolve more and more toward reliance on the financial criteria used by traditional firms.

The incentive system in an innovative subsidiary should serve two cardinal purposes. The first is to reward managers for energizing the feedback mechanisms that alert the firm to unanticipated problems and the subsidiary's ability to respond. The second is to reward managers for acting in ways consistent with basic, proinnovative strategies (for example, to strengthen the control system, to integrate functions, to encourage creativity, to enhance communication, and so forth).

One pitfall to this approach is that as the subsidiary grows and changes, managers may not adapt accordingly; however, this problem may be countered by routinely revising and reconfiguring the incentive system to be consonant with strategic imperatives as they evolve. Such reconfiguration, however, entails the imposition of subjective judgments, which some parties may perceive to be arbitrary or unfair.

Some innovative subsidiaries have countered this perception by actively soliciting the input of all managers, both in reconfiguring the incentive system and in evaluating their fellow managers. For example, a scientist who perfects a patent potentially vital to the subsidiary's success may receive overwhelming support from fellow managers for receiving a premium bonus; the next year, the marketing manager who successfully launches the product may receive peer approbation and the concomitant rewards.

Common to the incentive systems of nearly all the firms

surveyed was a reward scheme in which all managers could participate. While all key managers received salaries and occasional bonuses, they also hold a stake in the firm's future, in one of two ways. The first is through stock ownership. The second is through profit-sharing. The overall effect of such an incentive system is to ensure that a manager, by receiving a direct monetary benefit of firm-favoring behavior, will act to ensure the overall success of the firm.

SUMMARY

When moving from a defensive to a proactive strategy toward innovating abroad, subsidiaries must establish nontraditional control systems that are responsive and highly adaptable to sudden shifts in external conditions. Particularly in its early stages, the innovating subsidiary both must weather survival-threatening crises and overcome the debilitating effects of uncertainties endemic to innovating in foreign markets. Rather than designing fixed, goal-oriented control systems, as do traditional firms, innovating subsidiaries must design control systems that are highly flexible, driven by subjective evaluations of both internal and external forces, and geared to providing feedback about how best to readjust resources and priorities in response to crises and uncertainty. Lacking historical data and past operating experience with which to plan strategies to meet short- and longer-term goals, subsidiaries' control systems must serve as a surrogate tool with which to overcome those handicaps. This may seem a radically different approach, but considering the difficulties incumbent in an innovative endeavor abroad, it is a necessity.

Four examples are provided of how such a control system might work in preserving the flexibility and health of the subsidiary, in the areas of planning, budgeting, performance measurement, and incentive systems. Ideally, this control system also will enhance intercommunication among the four basic functions of a subsidiary: finance, R&D, manufacturing, and marketing/sales. Finally, such control systems cannot be bought in some prefabricated form; rather, they must be individually tailored to meet the specific needs and conditions of each innovating subsidiary.

It goes without saying that even with an entrepreneurial control system in place, managers still may err in ways that overturn its benefits. Misguided approaches to marketing or manufacturing may prove far more ruinous to a firm than a poorly implemented or relatively inflexible control system. Indeed, a casual sampling of failed firms that *had* instituted control systems indicated that misjudgments and miscalculations about markets, technologies, and strategic responses played a much greater role than did control systems. Even in successful firms with control systems, we discovered cumbersome or even mediocre systems that could have benefited greatly from improvements.

The objective of this analysis, however, is neither to criticize nor to reform how entrepreneurial control systems are, or are not, implemented in innovating subsidiaries. Rather, it seeks to identify and describe those aspects of entrepreneurial control systems that best seem to correlate with the success of an innovating subsidiary.

NOTE

1. Author interview.

6

Emergence of Organizational Entrepreneurs

Creative entrepreneurs are the mavericks especially of American business, and increasing in numbers in Europe. They are offshoots of the mainstream who operate apart from large corporations in small, independent groups. It is their very smallness, unencumbered by formalized organizational structures and driven by stringent performance criteria, which gives them the freedom to innovate with such astonishing success. As the United States struggles to countermand the inroads made by Japanese and Western European firms into areas once dominated by U.S. multinationals, creative entrepreneurs are proving an invaluable resource.

Yet despite the highly publicized successes of an An Wang or a Ray Kroc, there are scores upon scores of unheralded failures. Further, it is a fact of present-day business that many classes of innovations, particularly those aimed at a worldwide market and those that involve highly complex technologies (such as computers or aerospace or automobiles or electric generating stations), can only take place within large multinational corporations, which have the experience and resources needed to undertake such large-scale endeavors. Creative entrepreneurs are still vital to this process, but they tend to take a different form than in the small, start-up entrepreneurial firm; that is, they frequently are assembled into teams and work in a corporate context.

Large corporations, however, discourage precisely those qualities that creative entrepreneurs display in abundance:

creativity, flexibility, innovative daring. Indeed, many U.S. multinationals shy away from innovation abroad, preferring instead the relative security of maintaining current profit margins and market shares abroad, and focusing innovative activity on domestic markets. As demonstrated in Part I, many lack the motivations of sales abroad or competitive threats to innovate for foreign markets; still others lack the ingredients vital to successful innovation abroad, such as preestablished R&D and manufacturing facilities overseas, actual operating experience in those markets, conducive corporate structures, and so forth. And in the past two decades or so, foreign competition has seriously eroded the supremacy of the U.S. multinational's position in the world marketplace, and if American business concerns abroad are to "not go gently into that good night," then they must consider adopting elements of the entrepreneurial spirit and foster corporate and subsidiary environments in which innovation can thrive. Thus, a crucial consideration motivating the switch from a defensive to a proactive strategy for innovation abroad may entail the perception by U.S. multinationals that there are *opportunities* to innovate which, if foregone, may have repercussions beyond immediate issues of loss of sales or market share. Put bluntly, even those multinationals without a substantive, current, vested interest in foreign markets may discover that failure to innovate through subsidiaries abroad, whether or not they already have in place overseas R&D and manufacturing facilities, will have serious repercussions in the longer term. Such repercussions might include loss of *domestic* markets to foreign competitors, erosion of such intangible asset advantages as prestige and brand-name loyalty, and the atrophying of once-vital organizational structures and functions.

Some large U.S. corporations exhibit characteristics anathema to innovation. These include highly centralized structures for planning and decision making, entrenched bureaucracies, emphasis on long-term investments and preoccupation with short-term profits, nomadic middle and upper managements, and so forth. All these characteristics were evolved to serve logical and necessary purposes, and many of these purposes still exist today and should continue to do so for some time into the future. Thus, these corporations, particularly U.S. multi-nationals, are engaged in highly complex activities, such as coordinating the acquisition and transport of raw materials to points of manufacture; they operate in countries with often drastically different financial, labor, social, cultural, and legal conditions; and they must address market imperfections and uncertainties in a concerted and responsive fashion—all this, and keep stockholders happy as well. All these factors militate in favor of more centralized control and oversight. Yet, however true all this may be, the fact remains that large corporations are structured in such ways that are antithetical to innovation, and if innovation is a key to the future success and health of the U.S. multinational community, then ways must be found to do so in as least disruptive and as most productive a fashion as possible.

The most logical solution is also the most simple and inexpensive: to superimpose, integrate, and encourage the innovative vitality found in small, start-up entrepreneurial firms onto the structures of these larger, more traditional corporations. As we have seen, one fundamental mechanism by which to achieve this is through the establishment of innovation-oriented subsidiaries abroad, but this nonetheless also entails changes in attitude by parent corporations. Granted, changing the mind-set and psychology of any large institution is no simple matter, but if its value can be shown to be great and the disruptions and expenses proportionately modest, then the resulting motivation should be dynamic. Further, as initial successes accumulate, other corporations should find encouragement to follow down the same path, and over time a scanty trend may evolve into a full-fledged reorientation of strategy for innovating abroad. Undertaking a proactive strategy will require abstaining from the punishment of short-term failure and instead recognizing that failure many times contains hidden rewards; other tactics may involve deploying skunk works, shifting R&D resources more to subsidiaries abroad, reorienting parent corporate structures more to the geographical market approach, establishing flexible, individually-tailored control systems, and other methods enumerated throughout this book. Indeed, the surveys conducted by the author firmly suggest that U.S. multinationals which follow such strategies do experience significant increases in successful innovativeness.

Still, implementing such changes does not necessarily guarantee results, for one simple and overriding reason. Developing and managing innovation ultimately depends on the talents and intelligence of people. In small start-up companies, the creative entrepreneur usually is the motivating force behind an innovation, but in large corporations innovators are a somewhat different breed, here termed the "organizational entrepreneur."

Before turning to this subject, it is worthwhile to cite several results from the author's survey of those fifteen U.S. multinationals that successfully innovate abroad. The eight multinationals with identifiable organizational entrepreneurs are estimated to have developed fully one-third more innovations than those without them, and at a markedly faster rate. (The data do not attempt to weight the scale of complexity of those innovations; however, IBM's computer-related innovations, for example, may require more time and resources to develop than a new line of see-through cookware by Corning). A study of corporations in direct competition within the same industry, and having similar products and production capabilities, further indicates that those having organizational entrepreneurs outperformed those without them; similar results appeared even within firms. Among wholly-owned subsidiaries of U.S. multinationals that were highly R&D-intensive, those having identifiable organizational entrepreneurs generated 1.5 more innovations than did their counterparts.

That said, the discussion now turns to a description of organizational entrepreneurs.

ORGANIZATIONAL ENTREPRENEURS

In 1986, Howard H. Stevenson isolated six characteristics distinguishing organizational entrepreneurs (whom he terms "promoters") from trustees (conventionally-oriented corporate managers) in U.S. corporations with an innovative slant. These six characteristics are motivation, commitment to opportunity, strategic orientation, resources commitment, resources control, and concept of management.[1] To Stevenson's focus we include, where appropriate, comparisons with independent (that is, of small, start-up firms) entrepreneurs as well. Using these six characteristics as a general framework, we thus derive insight into what distinguishes an organizational entrepreneur's approach to innovation in a traditional corporate structure from those of both the corporate trustee and the independent entrepreneur, as well as identifying the potential hurdles an organizational entrepreneur faces and how he might overcome them.

Motivation

All entrepreneurs, whatever their classification, share one common trait: They are motivated by the conviction that the innovation will succeed. Taking this as a given, the motivations for an independent entrepreneur to innovate in some fundamental sense are as mysterious as those driving a Kandinsky to paint. On the other hand, most independent entrepreneurs are required, either by practical necessity or by their financial backers, to invest either personal financial resources or such "personal capital" as reputation or time in the innovations they have fostered. Thus, the expectation of some future gain—usually financial, but not necessarily—motivates the independent entrepreneur.

Organizational entrepreneurs face motivation-deadening obstacles that never burden independent entrepreneurs. Their corporate bosses high in the hierarchy may fail to see any potential benefits deriving from an innovation; a president or chairman three years from retirement himself might lack motivation to pursue an innovation proposed by an organizational entrepreneur. Or supportive managers might lack the authority to encourage an innovation, or perceive the risks of failure as potentially jeopardizing their own positions.

Organizational entrepreneurs are motivated by factors additional to personal gain, such as prestige, the acquisition of greater authority within the corporation, or peer recognition.

Organizational entrepreneurs also differ in how risk influences motivation. The independent entrepreneur frequently must invest a large degree of personal resources—either financial, reputational, or time—whereas the organizational entrepreneur invests *corporate* financial resources. Thus, the organizational entrepreneur may hedge risk in another way. When developing an innovation—particularly a highly technological or otherwise capital-intensive product—the organizational entrepreneur may choose to pull together a team, each member of which works collectively to develop an innovation. Again, the corporation bears the bulk of the financial risk, and personal, reputational risk may be seen as diffusing among the various members of the team.

Compensation/Reward Systems

Independent entrepreneurs, if successful, already have been awarded one primary objective: their inherent drive to innovate, to create, has borne fruit. If additional financial rewards are important, the independent entrepreneur can construct the firm in such ways as to glean monetary compensation. Likewise, if prestige or authority are paramount, the entrepreneur can work with financial backers to derive these compensations. Finally, if the fundamental attraction lies with the challenges and joys of innovation for innovation's sake, the independent entrepreneur can use either the new company's structure or the financial rewards derived from it to pursue that objective.

Organizational entrepreneurs who operate within large corporate structures, however, tend to be rewarded along more restrictive lines, and this works both to their and the corporation's disadvantage. As suggested in Chapter 5, control systems should restructure incentive systems and performance measures in ways that reward organizational entrepreneurs, *even if they fail.* Innovation is not a traditional business activity, particularly when it entails foreign markets, and it follows that using traditional standards to measure an organizational entrepreneur's performance might be distortive. Applying traditional standards to the trustee, however, may be applicable (or, if the trustee is involved with an organizational entrepreneur in pursuing an innovative opportunity, they may not be), but organizational entrepreneurs cannot be judged simply in

terms of how effectively they have reduced costs or met pro-
ductivity goals or increased short-term profit margins. Such
emphasis both ignores, and may fatally inhibit, the hit-or-miss,
groping-in-the-dark approach sometimes vital to the innovative process.

Some U.S. multinationals—and a host of small, start-up entrepreneurial firms—address this problem by instituting inventive ways to meet the financial expectations of the
organizational entrepreneur, at the same time they provide
motivations for success. Stock ownership in the innovating subsidiary is one example; generous buy-out agreements are another; the awarding of substantial monetary or stock bonuses,
or the transfer of patent ownership or licensing rights are yet
others.

However responsive these arrangements might be in some
cases, they mean nothing when an organizational entrepreneur
fails in an innovative endeavor—fails in the sense the innovation either is never developed, or collapses at some stage
prior to commercialization. Here the suggestions proposed in
Chapter 5 must come into play. It being understood that even
a failed attempt to innovate may later yield invaluable side-
benefits, one way to reward an organizational entrepreneur for
failure might be to solicit the input of manager and staff closely
associated with the effort. Under certain circumstances, the
benefits accruing from a failure might not become apparent for
some time; in these cases, rewards might be made retroactively
if the organizational entrepreneur had left the firm, or even
posthumously. Granted, such compensation systems rely upon
highly subjective criteria and accurate, quantifiable judgments
might be far and few between, but pursuing such an approach
would serve two purposes: from the organizational entrepreneur's point of view, it would be just; and from the corporation's
point of view, it would signal to *all* employees its iron commitment to innovation and its understanding of the complex-
ities of the process.

Strategic Orientation

Organizational entrepreneurs and trustees both pursue radically different strategies to reach their goals within the cor-

porate structure. An organizational entrepreneur, seeing an opportunity to develop an innovation, focuses on achieving the end product; a trustee, on the other hand, focuses on conserving and preserving corporate resources. One is change-oriented; the other is conservative. Although the two approaches may be diametrically opposed, and frequently are, no criticism is implied; each is simply doing his job as defined by the corporation.

To be truly effective, the organizational entrepreneur must fuse elements of the trustee's approach if he is to see an innovation developed within the corporate context. Thus, the organizational entrepreneur must evaluate an opportunity in terms of the demands and stresses it would place on corporate resources. With rare exceptions, he or she pursues only those innovation opportunities that are consistent with overall corporate strategy (one would not develop a Cabbage Patch Kid at General Motors, for example, no matter how promising the market). However, in context of subsidiaries abroad, the organizational entrepreneur may enjoy considerably greater freedom and independence from the corporate parent.

It is generally true that the organizational entrepreneur displays far greater flexibility in strategic orientation than does the trustee. For example, if there are constraints on internal corporate resources, the organizational entrepreneur may feel free to seek creative solutions by drawing upon external resources, such as hiring consultants or contracting-out certain activities. The trustee, on the other hand, acts through conventional channels and focuses on utilizing corporate resources already in place.

In sum, the organizational entrepreneur serves two masters simultaneously—innovation and the corporation—whereas the trustee obeys corporate dictates more exclusively. These are in marked contrast to the independent entrepreneur, who, not limited by any established corporate strategy, is relatively free to pursue or abandon innovation opportunities.

Commitment to Opportunities

Peter Drucker provides an amusing, if dated, illustration of how an opportunity to develop an innovation might appear from left field. In 1909, a statistician for AT&T, whose name is lost to posterity, projected the growth of telephone traffic and correlated it with projections of U.S. population growth fifteen years into the future. From the resulting numbers he concluded, presumably with some dismay, that by the year 1920, nearly *every single female* in the United States would have to be employed as a switchboard operator to handle increased demand for telephones. And in 1909, faced with apocalyptic projections, a manager for AT&T, whose name is also lost to posterity, recognized the pressing need to develop an innovation that would forestall this massive realignment in U.S. employment needs. The result? AT&T went on to develop the automatic telephone switchboard.[2]

The foregoing anecdote not only indicates that opportunities to innovate may surface from the most unlikely of waters, but that it is the crucial job of an organizational entrepreneur to recognize and seize upon them. Although not then called an "organizational entrepreneur," this unnamed AT&T manager was performing precisely that function, and his role in the longer term proved crucial to the success of his company. In fact, Drucker argues that most successful innovations do not "spring from a flash of genius," but rather result "from a conscious, purposeful search for ... opportunities."[3] The author's survey supports this contention, and if true, the fact throws even greater importance upon the presence of organizational entrepreneurs in the intracorporate innovation process.

That said, a few words about *commitment* to opportunity are in order. Once an organizational entrepreneur has identified an opportunity, received corporate support, and committed corporate resources to developing an innovation, this marks only the *beginning* of his relationship to the process, for it is the job of an organizational entrepreneur to follow an innovation through various stages over a period of time, up to and including commercialization. If the trustee also is committed, he too must commit to pursuit of the opportunity over a period of time. Presumably the greater and deeper the amount of resources committed, the less likely it is that the innovation will be aborted midstream.

Independent entrepreneurs, however, because they undertake innovation with substantially sparser resources, may feel freer to abandon an opportunity or a particular route toward innovating. It is not that their degree of commitment is less—as explained in the previous section on motivation, both groups of entrepreneurs have strong personal stakes in the success of an innovation—but that for resource and structural reasons, they may possess greater flexibility vis-à-vis innovation opportunities. This leads us directly to the fifth point.

Commitment of Resources

By virtue of working within a large U.S. multinational, the organizational entrepreneur, in having chosen to pursue a particular opportunity to innovate, has at his or her disposal potentially substantial financial, personnel, R&D, and other resources, both internal and external. On the other hand, the independent entrepreneur might discover that he or she must devote substantial time and energy in searching for the appropriate resources. For example, an independent entrepreneur might need to devote months of substantial effort in approaching potential investors before receiving financial assistance. Further, the independent entrepreneur must develop a coherent and persuasive business plan and supporting documentation; none of these are trivial efforts. The organizational entrepreneur, assuming he or she has secured the backing of the corporation, can bypass many of these headaches.

Further, by virtue of the fact that he or she controls only limited resources—both financial and personnel—the independent entrepreneur finds that available resources must be committed on an as-needed basis, in response to short-term crises, rather than having resources allocated from a fixed, known, and reliable pool to serve activities further into the future. This necessity of independent entrepreneurs to "jerry-rig," although it might give them some flexibility in committing or abandoning opportunities, has a detrimental side effect: The sequencing of resource commitments over a multistage process is usually more economically efficient in the longer term, and independent entrepreneurs are unable to capture these advantages.

Trustees, of course, view independent entrepreneurs as existing in a continually undercapitalized state, which makes them imprudent in their business behavior and renders them fiscally vulnerable. Trustees operate under a much longer-term planning horizon, and in interacting within the corporate structure with organizational entrepreneurs, they are likely to use their influence to help the organizational entrepreneur gain the resource-sequencing advantages unavailable to the independent entrepreneur.

Once again the organizational entrepreneur strives to combine crucial aspects of both his or her independent entrepreneur counterpart and the corporate trustee to whom he or she must answer. That is, the organizational entrepreneur wishes both to capture some of the independent entrepreneur's flexibility as well as obeying the trustee's more rational, effective approach to resource allocation. In order to do this, the organizational entrepreneur views as crucial how corporate resources are *controlled,* and since in a large corporation trustees have primary authority over this area their relationship with organizational entrepreneurs becomes critical, as the following discussion shows.

Control of Resources

In the typical U.S. multinational, a trustee manages the disposition of an abundance of resources, in whatever form, and the trustee's performance, prestige, and power are measured in terms of how well he or she manages these resources (return on investments, cost overruns, manufacturing economies of scale, and so forth). As we have seen, the innovation process tends to be a relatively risky endeavor and the trustee tends to be an inherently conservative creature; thus, if the trustee's function is to oversee the progress of an innovation under stewardship of a given organizational entrepreneur, there inherently exists a possible conflict between the two groups, one with potentially enormous repercussions for the trustee and one to which the organizational entrepreneur must be acutely sensitive.

One way to illuminate this potential conflict is to state that a creative entrepreneur places primary weight upon the opportunity to innovate, and only secondly asks how the necessary resources might be secured. The trustee, presented with an organizational entrepreneur's request for resources, is primarily concerned with (a) whether there are better alternative ways to deploy those resources, and (b) how most efficiently and conservatively to allocate them.

The responsive and responsible organizational entrepreneur, once again finding himself serving two masters (the innovation and the corporation in which it will be developed), must balance the needs of both without denying the exigencies of either. Such organizational entrepreneurs may take one of three tacts, and preferably all of them simultaneously. First, he may "sculpt" the innovation opportunity to match available resources; that is, he must explicitly gear development to take place in discrete stages, the failure of any one of which will terminate the process. Second, and equally vital, he must work *with* the trustee both to educate that trustee as to alternative ways to deploy resources and to sensitize himself as to the pressures bearing upon the trustee. Third, in no event will the savvy organizational entrepreneur pursue an innovation opportunity if the new technology or product falls outside the realm of corporate objectives or if the effort requires (at least in its early stages) resources either beyond those the corporation possesses or is likely to commit. For instance, the organizational entrepreneur and the trustee may together decide that it is more fiscally responsible to rely upon supplementary (external) resources, either when they are unavailable within the corporation or when they are too expensive to shift from existing tasks to the innovative undertaking. Or contrarily, perhaps guided by the knowledgeable trustee, the organizational entrepreneur may deploy corporate resources that are currently being underused, seizing advantage of slack capacity in ways that are not objectionable to the trustee, and then freely release control over those resources either when they are needed elsewhere, when the opportunity has diminished or altered, or when they have accomplished their task. By employing such types of approaches, the organizational entrepreneur can find ways to approach the flexibilities enjoyed by the independent entrepreneur at the same time he or she works in coordination with the corporation's constraints and objectives. The simplicity or ingenuity of solutions will always depend upon the nature of the particular innovation, the degree of rigidity of the trustee and/or corporation, the availability of resources, and so forth, but in all cases the organizational entrepreneur must derive diplomatic, rational, and perhaps creative solutions that serve both the innovation opportunity and the strictures of the corporation.

These approaches to resource control of course also vary depending upon the corporation's management structure. An organizational entrepreneur with full authority over, say, a foreign subsidiary's activities would have drastically fewer conflicts than one operating in, say, the domestic headquarters of a U.S. multinational inexperienced in innovating abroad. At present, however, most organizational entrepreneurs operate more in the latter than in the former mode, and thus the following section is cast more toward that context.

Concept of Management Structure

The independent entrepreneur's concept of management structure could be said to be analogous to Wassily Kandinsky's improvisational approach to Abstract Expressionism. Kandinsky held that art was best served by rendering form (structure) subservient to content (the innovation); that is, content determines form, and to impose form upon content acts to restrict the spirituality and spontaneity of art. Analogously, the independent entrepreneur holds that the nature of the innovation determines the management structure overseeing generation of that innovation; indeed, structure evolves to serve innovation.

However, the organizational entrepreneur, by virtue of acting within the confines of a preestablished corporate structure, enjoys no such luxury. Traditionally, corporations and particularly U.S. multinationals are structured to achieve specific, well-defined goals. Each stratum, each division, and each department of the corporate organization exists to accomplish a specific task, and all strata work in concert to achieve the common corporate goal. A manufacturing division manufactures products; a sales division markets them. Whereas the independent entrepreneur must experiment with solutions to conditions and crises as they arise—an approach hardly conducive to creating a highly hierarchical and authoritarian structure—the organizational entrepreneur must foster an innovation within context of an existing management structure.

The trustee, as guardian of corporate resources and goals, obeys the strictures of a highly-defined chain of authority designed to accomplish tasks in a routine and orderly way. Fluidity gives way to something more rigid; the trustee understands that a corporation would become quickly insolvent if each manager experimented with new approaches at will.

The organizational entrepreneur again strives to combine elements of both management concepts. Although he or she may belong to a corporation that affords proinnovation flexibility, ultimately the organizational entrepreneur still must obey the dictates of the corporate hierarchy. Some subsidiaries of large U.S. multinationals, however, are constructed so as to act autonomously of the corporate parent, in which case the organizational entrepreneur will enjoy most of the same freedom of flexibility available to the independent entrepreneur. For instance, U.S. multinationals increasingly are establishing venture capital subsidiaries that operate independently of the parent. The head of the venture capital subsidiary reports to the parent only on broad financial and operational matters; otherwise he or she is free to innovate according to foreign-market demands and to deploy resources accordingly. Although subsidiaries so structured are relatively uncommon, there is a burgeoning trend in this direction. (It should be noted that as regards venture capital subsidiaries, the parent corporation usually has explicitly chosen to support an innovative project that may or may not conform to its overall corporate strategy, and thus has willingly foregone the imposition of strategic constraints that might otherwise be present.)

Most organizational entrepreneurs, however, must innovate within the strictures of traditionally structured corporations, and so the challenge entails how to operate up and down the parent hierarchical chain. In this regard the organizational entrepreneur must display a unique managerial attribute: the ability to manage skillfully both subordinates and superiors, some of whom may have little vested interest in innovation. To do so successfully may require a Kissingerian genius for diplomacy, an ability to find common grounds where none appear on the surface. In a sense, the organizational entrepreneur must manage those persons ostensibly empowered to manage *him* or *her*. In practical application, the effective organizational entrepreneur is sometimes aided in this challenge by developing a pupil-mentor relationship with a superior. In this relationship, ideas and approaches are discussed freely and openly, without risk of penalty, and if an innovative project receives a green light from the corporation, the organizational entrepreneur receives the protection of this mentor (a relationship not unlike that between an independent entrepreneur and his or her financial backers).

In summary, the organizational entrepreneur once again fuses two concepts of management structure that are, on the surface, in theoretical opposition. That is, he or she acts within the confines of the existing and hierarchical corporate structure at the same time seeking to eke out flexibility to serve the innovative process. If serving in an independent, proinnovative subsidiary, these dichotomies will be less prevalent, but in any event, the organizational entrepreneur's concept of management structure entails the fusion of both the flexibility required by innovation and the obedience to corporate hierarchical demands.

Drawing upon the preceding description of the characteristics of organizational entrepreneurs and of their specific problems and potential approaches to innovation within a large corporate setting, we now turn to the crucial issue of how U.S. multinationals wishing to pursue a proactive strategy to innovation abroad might act to foster organizational entrepreneurs. A brief recitation of structural issues sets the stage for the discussion.

STRUCTURAL BARRIERS TO INNOVATION

Although some managers extol the virtues of innovation in public, in private their actions bespeak a conservative belief that innovation in fact is destabilizing and costly (particularly in corporations belonging to an oligopoly). Destabilizing because they create the potential for new market entrants, and costly because, if they fail, the financial loss is seen to be total. Managers in follower firms are particularly cautious in this regard, justifying their reluctance to innovate in terms of the overriding exigencies of the overall corporate strategy. This creativity-stifling attitude readily transfers from top management down the ladder to the bulk of employees, many of whom, by being intimately involved in the daily operations of the corporation, are precisely those best situated to develop useful innovations in the first place.

Such entrenched attitudes have repercussions beyond the immediate failure to innovate. A multinational that has not structurally and psychologically removed the barriers to innovation may well find itself unable to respond readily to competitive threats, when eventually they do arise. Further, talented and innovation-oriented managers will shy away from corporations known for conservative stances. Thus, the failure to foster innovation carries a potential cost that may become manifest only in the *future*.

Follower Firms, Innovation, and the Short Term

By nature and definition, follower firms in an oligopoly flourish best in times of *stability;* innovation being perceived as anathema to stability, their overall strategy is restricted to one of imitation. The author's survey confirms this tendency, finding that follower firms did not nurture (or value) organizational entrepreneurs nearly to the extent leader firms did. There is a clear trade-off: stability for innovation. This strategy is understandable in oligopolies based on mature technologies where the threat of competition is minimal, but recent encroachment by the Japanese and Western Europeans suggests that the concept of "mature technologies" may in fact be chimerical: as witness the U.S. automobile, steel-making, and electronics industries.

On the other hand, if imitative firms indeed undertake radical innovations, there is a clear and present risk that such actions will destabilize the overall structure of the oligopoly. In such event, losers will far outstrip winners. And, of course, if an imitative firm fails in an effort to innovate, it may provoke serious punitive reaction by both leader firms and fellow imitators. In short, follower firms may be "damned if they do, and damned if they don't." As hoary as this Catch–22 may be, it is a Catch–22 that exists in the short term only. Survival belongs to the long term, and innovation is oriented to the future.

Innovation and the Long Term

Decisions about innovation, if made with an eye only to the short term, are doomed to serve only the short term; and at this moment in history, now more than ever, short- and long-term business strategies are at serious odds. Foreign competition and foreign innovation will not simply vanish overnight, leaving American corporations to play the part of followers, picking up the market crumbs left behind. Innovation has become *the* rule of the game, and innovation, which is a dynamic process, obeys certain laws unto itself.

One of these guiding laws is that a corporation's structural and psychological receptiveness to innovation determines what kind of employees it attracts as managers. The author's survey of corporate personnel directors supports this point: New applicants who are innovation-oriented gravitate to positions in corporations with a history of innovation at a rate perhaps twice as high as in those follower firms that did not. The point is not to be taken lightly: As U.S. multinationals become increasingly interested in innovating abroad, competition for organizational entrepreneurs will become increasingly fierce. U.S. multinationals that persevere in hiring "imitative" managers will find themselves bound into an unretractable strategy wholly unsuited to withstanding the unpredictable whirlwinds of technological innovation. And, further, the *size* of such corporations may become less and less a factor, as smaller but more innovative firms find themselves able to pay the salaries and to offer the other compensations once reserved exclusively for the giants.

Given all this, large U.S. multinationals would do well to

consider building a network of organizational entrepreneurs over a sustained period of time, beginning now. Their organizational and compensation structures should be redesigned in a way attractive to innovation-oriented managers. And top management should identify and encourage such individuals already present in their organizations, recognizing and rewarding them as an indispensable asset. The alternative to such an approach by the American corporate community may well be that *all* U.S. corporations will become follower firms, doomed to playing second banana to foreign counterparts. The cost of trying is trivial compared with the cost of trying nothing.

FOSTERING ORGANIZATIONAL ENTREPRENEURS

A number of concrete suggestions as how best to foster organizational entrepreneurs within a corporate setting are embodied in Chapter 5 and in the above discussion, particularly regarding issues of performance evaluation and compensation/reward systems. Here several additional approaches are presented.

Organizational entrepreneurs of the talent and vigor of an An Wang or Bill Land are rare as seed oysters in Switzerland, and infinitely more precious. A vital question is: Does increased innovation result from refashioning structures and instituting new incentive systems, or from the direct intellectual and creative contributions of certain individuals? The answer, once again, is not one or the other, but a dynamic combination of both. Just as a young musical prodigy can never achieve the brilliance of an Isaac Stern without access to a professionally constructed violin, a U.S. multinational that does not provide, say, true organizational flexibility cannot expect to foster organizational entrepreneurs for innovation abroad with any real degree of success. Thus, inducing those *structural* characteristics identified with heightened innovation does not necessarily assure that the corporation will achieve anything other than heightened structural confusion. Structural and other changes will not succeed unless they emanate from the sincere conviction of top management.

In the author's survey of twenty-five U.S. multinationals, fifteen were found to have made a concerted attempt to foster innovation, many by initiating "skunk works" or following the team approach. Yet, despite these endeavors, managers could not offer persuasive evidence that heightened informativeness resulted. Why? Because, according to interviews with managers of those fifteen firms, these changes were merely cosmetic, failing to bear fruit because they did not have the wholehearted support of top management. Rather than vigorously supporting an atmosphere conducive to innovation, top management instead erected only a cardboard facade. One manager described his corporation's approach as "putting a streamlined body around a V–6 engine," and another as "putting a Ferrari body on a Fiat chassis."[4] The point is well taken: cosmetic changes do not help cars win auto races.

Thus, managers themselves agree that a vital ingredient in nurturing organizational entrepreneurs is a proinnovation environment established and supported by top management. In part this is true because weak advocacy seldom will overcome traditionally-held emphasis on achieving short-term goals or pursuing risk-averse strategies. In such cases, potential organizational entrepreneurs remain submerged in the corporation, discouraged by the antithetical priorities of top management, and sooner or later they can be expected to seek out pastures more receptive and appreciative of their particular class of managerial skills.

Of the ten firms identified in the above survey as having frequent innovations, their managers estimated that the number of visible, widely acknowledged organizational entrepreneurs ranged between three and five per firm (incidentally the same number cited by managers of the other fifteen firms for persons having the *potential* to become organizational entrepreneurs). This suggests that there is no paucity of talent available. It further suggests that there is room for improvement, even among innovating corporations; three to five seems a modest number, although others may be hidden from sight and operating somewhat behind-the-scenes. In any case, the point should be made that organizational entrepreneurs could well occupy not just top but also middle management positions. And, in the best of all possible worlds, an organization *primarily* devoted to innovation (such as certain foreign subsidiaries, say) would benefit from *all* employees, whatever their rank, acting as organizational entrepreneurs. (The "Pathfinders" example from 3M, to be explained shortly, is an excellent illustration of this point.)

Among those corporations with only shaky confidence or commitment to innovation, there is a Catch–22 at work. Top managers in such firms often cite their manifest lack of faith in middle management's ability to encourage innovation, as a primary factor in discouraging their efforts to take action themselves. Having no motivation to institute, for example, a reconceptualization of incentive systems designed to foster and reward organizational entrepreneurs, they are stymied by the paradox. Their manifest lack of faith in manager's abilities to innovate then tends to perpetrate the view that their firms cannot innovate with the same efficiency as their competitors. Either tact, whether supportive or indifferent to innovation, thus tends to be self-fulfilling. The deadlock can be broken *only* by positive action by top management, and as we have tried to suggest here, such action can be taken through means that are both relatively inexpensive and nondisruptive.

In addition to support from top management, some U.S. multinationals that are successful in innovating reveal another characteristic: All individual employees, from CEO to nightshift maintenance crew, perceive that their contributions are vital to the well-being of the corporation. As pride of belonging translates into enthusiasm for work, activities take on a creative and unique aspect, and corporations that foster such a spirit will find ideas for innovation, whether of process or product, emerging from the unlikeliest of places.

An example illustrates. An Exxon employee at the Baytown, Texas, refinery, working on his own time, designed several tools that allowed a single individual, rather than the customary two, to inspect on-site holding tanks.[5] However seemingly modest this innovation might appear on the surface, it cut both inspection time and direct labor costs by 50 percent, and has the further, unquantifiable side-benefit of encouraging other employees to take similar initiatives. Thus, the domain of innovation belongs not just to top research scientists and manufacturing process engineers, but to all employees. Minor as the echo-bells in Berlioz's *Symphonie fantastique* may seem to be, their absence would cause the entire third movement to collapse.

The "Pathfinders" program, instituted in 1978 by 3M Corporation, provides a second excellent example.[6] In an effort to foster innovative thinking in 3M, the company each year votes a substantial financial award to an employee or group of employees who develop an innovation that has the potential of generating at least $150,000 in sales at a reasonable level of profit. "Pathfinder" awards may devolve upon an employee from *any* division of the company, either domestically- or foreign-based. (A similar program, called "Circle of Excellence," is geared exclusively to R&D laboratory employees.) Further, Pathfinder award recipients are then given the opportunity to pursue that innovation through to actual commercialization, with full corporate support. According to one 3M manager, 3M "lives or dies on innovation," and the Pathfinders program is only one example of this corporate philosophy.

The idea is to foster an "innovation-friendly" atmosphere throughout the width and breadth of the corporation, including overseas subsidiaries. We can't "force-feed" some products to a foreign market; the market must determine the product. Japanese companies operate under an inherent handicap because, despite popular perceptions to the contrary, their managements are highly autocratic, and autocracy inhibits creativity. This is why Japanese firms, again contrary to popular perception, tend to engage more in incremental than radical innovating; the same holds for U.K. firms. You see, we really believe this; we pay much more than lip service to innovation. There is an entire corporately-supported structure underlying this belief in innovation, and it works like this. Any 3M employee, whether here in the United States or based somewhere abroad, is encouraged to interact with any other 3M division anywhere in the world when he or she is in pursuit of an innovative idea. They are encouraged to draw upon whatever intercorporate expertise they feel they might need, whether it means talking to marketing people or manufacturing experts or top-notch R&D technicians. The company picks up any related travel expenses, and assists in arranging meetings among interested parties. It's a highly informal approach, this scheme we've constructed to encourage technology development, because we firmly believe that more structured approaches inhibit innovations. We encourage free and easy communication instead. Flexible, informal. And if the risk of tackling an innovation is high, so be it; the pay-off can be ten times as high. Employee enthusiasm is worth one thousand three-hundred page reports; you can't buy enthusiasm. That's why the Pathfinder awards are made by top, top management. That signals to the whole family of employees that commitment to innovation originates at the top and permeates the whole company's structure.

Let me give another example, humble as it might be. A bunch of guys in our Swedish subsidiary came up with the idea of a cardboard frame for transparencies, those sheets of plastic used in overhead projections. They figured these frames would both cut down on the projector light shining into the user's eyes, and would give space for the user to jot notes, figures, whatever. The idea's humble, okay, but that's not the point. The point is that the idea originated in Sweden, the cardboard frames were manufactured in one of our U.S. facilities, and it was marketed throughout Europe and in the United States alike. The point is that this cross-cultural interaction, if you will, is utterly supportive of 3M's belief in wide-open communication throughout the entire company. Encouraging innovation is great, fine, but there have to be ways to support it. Lots of ways. And we think that we have those lots of ways, and we're always open to others. I guess you *can* teach an old dog new tricks.[7]

One observation about the above quotation begs to be made. Whatever the expenses involved in actually undertaking an innovation, the corporate mechanisms that act in support of an innovative spirit among employees—awards, informal communication, travel—are *not* expensive. They are more attitudinal in nature, and it costs nothing to change an attitude.

NOTES

1. Howard H. Stevenson and William Sahlman. "Entrepreneurship: A Process, Not a Person." Harvard University Graduate School of Business Administration Paper no. 87–09, 1987.

2. Peter F. Drucker. "The Discipline of Innovation," in *Harvard Business Review,* May/June 1985, p. 70.

3. Drucker, "The Discipline of Innovation," p. 67.

4. Author's interviews with managers of U.S. multinationals, proprietary.

5. Author's interview with manager of a U.S. multinational, proprietary.

6. Author's interview with 3M manager, proprietary.

7. Author's interview with 3M manager, proprietary.

Venturing Abroad: The Managerial Perspective

Any business, whether a Mom-and-Pop dry cleaners down the street or a multibillion dollar corporation sprawling the globe, whether a small start-up entrepreneurial firm or a complex corporate subsidiary innovating abroad, will eventually succeed or fail depending upon the actions of its managers. Also true is the fact that different types of business endeavors require different kinds of managers. Although the old, apocryphal story of the night-shift charwoman who wins $50 million in the Irish sweepstakes and subsequently leveraged buy-outs of her corporate employer may appeal to our secret dreams of retribution, in reality she probably would not make an effective Charperson of the Board.

As demonstrated in foregoing chapters, a business geared to innovation is very different from one with a more traditional orientation. Innovation at its heart is a creative activity, and creativity presents a host of unique problems whatever the endeavor. For instance, a start-up entrepreneurial firm here in the United States may find in its early stages that the crusty old entrepreneurial inventor, eccentric and brilliant as a Thomas Edison, may successfully serve as midwife, wetnurse, and mother to his product. That is, he not only conceives the innovation, but goes on to deliver and nurture it from infancy into early adulthood as well. Examples abound of crusty old inventors who went on to become crafty old businessmen, but so too do examples of crusty old entrepreneurs who, once their innovation had seen the light of day, then returned to the drafting table, leaving the day-to-day managerial tasks to others more skilled in those practical arts than themselves.

Managing innovation abroad through the subsidiary of a U.S. multinational likewise poses challenges, and under conditions quite unlike any others. All U.S. multinationals, to greater or lesser degree, are inherently rigid: by virtue of age, of structure, of consistency of focus, of historical necessity. Rigidity deplores change, yet change is the core dynamic that underlies innovation. Given this fundamental and antithetical opposition between the traditional U.S. multinational and the exigencies of innovation, and given the enormous obstacles of uncertainty and competition any innovative endeavor faces, where does the manager who can manage these traumas and this paradox come from, Mars? Such managers must be capable of drawing nurture from, and returning it to, two entirely different worlds; they must serve two masters: the parent corporation and the innovating subsidiary, tradition and newness.

These roles may be divided between two separate people, each with separate functions but both acting to serve the same goal: the visionary entrepreneur and the executor entrepreneur. And this indeed is the tack most frequently taken. *All* innovations need a mad creator, whether a dyslexic, sleep-starved Edison or a team of brainy, other-worldly scientists slaving away in some isolated laboratory among the debris of smashed atoms and spiraling strands of DNA. That is a given. Whether that mad parent of innovation is a single soul or a group of them, whether birth takes place before a drafting board in some rural Canadian township or in a corporate R&D lab or in a Bengali basement or in a Sao Paulo conference room does not really matter: throughout this book, the presence of a creator has been a given. Without a creator, there is no innovation. Our interest here instead lies with the *executor* of that innovation, the person or group of persons who manage that squalling, mewling infant of an innovation and see that it survives and thrives in an environment essentially hostile to it.

Accordingly, this chapter undertakes what in many ways is both the penultimate and most difficult aspect of U.S. multinationals shifting from a defensive to a proactive strategy:

Of the dual-oriented firms managed by visionary entrepreneurs (five out of twenty-two), survey results indicate that these five visionary entrepreneurs perceived radically new applications for technologies previously developed, and established those new businesses to apply those technologies. In four out of the five instances, they also founded the very first firms in their respective market niches. Further, in all five cases, the visionary entrepreneurs were themselves responsible for developing the innovative technology underlying the company.

The seventeen executor entrepreneurs heading dual-oriented firms uniformly cited that the execution or strategy was far more crucial than the original innovation in the firm's success. Most indicated that they either were duplicating an established innovation or addressing a market niche apparent to other competitions in their respective industries.

Of the financially-oriented firms having visionary entrepreneurs at their head (four out of eleven), all indicated that they were attempting to refashion those firms either to develop new, team-derived innovations geared for a specific market segment or were attempting to redefine the firm's basic strategy to capture new market shares. Mechanisms included leveraged buyouts as a means of financing entry into that industry, and in all four cases they exhibited both visionary and executor characteristics. The distinction resides in the fact that these four entrepreneurs perceived opportunities no other firms had perceived—their "visionary" contribution—whereas the seven executor entrepreneurs perceived opportunities to exploit market areas subject to existing competition.

Implications

These survey results yield two implications regarding relationship between class of entrepreneur and class of firm.

First, team-oriented firms, as suggested in Chapter 4, tend to group more in nascent industries (like computer, biotech, or chemical), or in industries in which a sudden new demand either arises or can be created (development of any variety of chemotherapies for a broad variety of cancers). As these firms evolve toward product development and ultimately production

describing this new sort of manager. Drawing upon a body of existing research, the chapter first distinguishes between the two fundamental types of organizational entrepreneurs—the visionary and the executor—and relates each to the three classes of innovating subsidiary first presented in Chapter 4. The chapter concludes with a set of specific recommendations for managers proactively innovating abroad.

Although the discussion is subjective and speculative, so too is the process of innovating for markets abroad, and concrete approaches are suggested only with the *caveat* that, as elsewhere in this book, it is imperative to design concrete approaches that are both dynamic and flexible. And equally as important, the shift from a defensive to a proactive strategy requires the construction of approaches tailored not just to meet the specific needs of each individual multinational and foreign market, but that respect and support this new class of managers.

VISIONARY VERSUS EXECUTOR ENTREPRENEURS

Managers of innovation-oriented businesses, whether a small, domestically-based start-up firm or a foreign-based subsidiary of a large U.S. multinational, fall into two distinct categories: the visionary entrepreneur, whose role primarily is to "invent" the innovation, and the executor entrepreneur, whose role is to take that innovation from conceptualization, drawing board, or prototype and see it through all intermediary stages to actual commercialization.

Although many organizational entrepreneurs indeed follow an innovation from birth through marketing and even beyond, this requirement is by no means absolute. In some cases the organizational entrepreneur's useful participation may terminate with development of a proven-marketable prototype, the commercialization of which then devolves to existing corporate/subsidiary divisions and their respective managers. In actual practice, feedback from a control system may help to determine at what points the organizational entrepreneur surrenders authority over the innovative process; but in any case, the length and emphasis of his participation will likely shift from case to case. Some organizational entrepreneurs may keep their fingers in many pies at many stages; others may serve more exclusively as troubleshooters; still others may follow the innovation through and past commercialization, even devoting an entire career to one single effort. Which obtains depends upon the personality of the individual organizational entrepreneur; to force an organizational entrepreneur to act beyond his own perceived commitment to an innovation may well result in his seeking opportunities elsewhere. Some degree of corporate flexibility, as always, is beneficial.

Most research into business imitators has focused upon broad traits of entrepreneurs. This research suggests that the archetypical entrepreneur tends to come from first- or second-generation immigrant families of only modest or even low incomes. More salient, they are found to exhibit traits commonly associated with "type-A" personalities. They are outgoing by nature, prone to take direct action rather than to labor decisions through reflective thought, and demonstrate a high tolerance for ambiguity or uncertainty; their motivation and sense of self-esteem derives from achieving externally- rather than internally-oriented goals; and they are moderate to high risk-takers. While it is admittedly tenuous to categorize people in such fashion, this description nonetheless reflects a consensus of the research into the personality of entrepreneurs.

During several years of investigation both into start-up entrepreneurial firms in the United States and into U.S. multinationals innovating through subsidiaries abroad, the author found subjective but persuasive indications that executor entrepreneurs tend to exhibit the same fundamental character traits as visionary entrepreneurs, but with one important difference: Each class of entrepreneur is associated with a specific stage that an innovative endeavor is in (refer to discussion of Chapter 4).

Thus, visionary entrepreneurs are most commonly associated with the technology monopoly stage, wherein attempts tend to focus primarily upon developing a radically new idea, technology, or product. Executor entrepreneurs, on the other hand, tend to be associated with firms in the product or service stages.

Tabl
Relation between Types of Company and Orienta

Types of Companies	Visionary	Executor	Total
Team	15	2	17
Concept	5	17	22
Financial	4	7	11
Totals	24	26	50

Source: Survey of 50 start-up firms

There may be a chicken/egg question at work here—tha visionary entrepreneurs gravitate more toward breakt innovations because that is where their specific tale needed, or do their specific talents lead determinist develop breakthrough innovations? The question ho wise for executor entrepreneurs.

Two Classes of Entrepreneurs, Three Cl Innovatir

Table 7.1, which draws upon the author's survey of up entrepreneurial firms in the United States, corr two classes of entrepreneur with the three classes of presented in Chapter 4 (technology monopoly/team dual, and service/financial). Survey results suggest oriented firms tend to be managed by visionary entr (fifteen versus two, or 88 percent); dual-oriented fi ecutor entrepreneurs (seventeen versus five, or 77 pe financially-oriented firms again by executor ent (seven versus four, or 66 percent).

Further examination proves revealing. Of the tea firms with executor entrepreneurs at their head seventeen), both firms were foundering toward ban thus would logically benefit more from the leader sionary than an executor entrepreneur.

and marketing, their managements show a demonstrable shift from the visionary to the executor entrepreneur.

This may occur for a variety of reasons. The founding father of an innovative company—duPont and General Motors are classic examples—either no longer wishes or is unable to handle the shift from an innovative to an administrative focus. The visionary entrepreneur, either by his own request or that of the firm's financial backers or board of directors, may surrender control over administrative activities to head the firm's R&D laboratories or, as with Steven Jobs of Apple, may retain only nominal participation in the original firm and pursue other innovations.

Analogously, executor entrepreneurs gravitate toward management more of dual (product) or financial (service) firms (although—particularly in large U.S. multinationals—it is not illogical that an executor entrepreneur would participate to limited extent in a team-oriented approach, with the visionary entrepreneur determining the core nature and thrust of the innovative effort and the executor entrepreneur acting more in managerial support of that effort). Again, however, once either a product- or service-oriented firm has become successful, and as the challenges of managing a new business give way to the more routinized, less dynamic needs of a steadily-growing company, the executor entrepreneur may choose to leave the firm in preference for more untested waters. In some cases the executor entrepreneur, particularly if he is the primary motivational force behind bringing a breakthrough innovation to prominence in a given industry, may be elevated in the corporate hierarchy to initiate or oversee other innovative efforts.

The second implication derives from the first, and is supported by the author's survey of U.S. multinationals innovating abroad. As intuition might suggest, the majority of successful firms tend to see in their early stages the linking-up of visionary with executor entrepreneurs. The earlier this happens, the more probable success will be (assuming the innovation is viable). Likewise, the executor entrepreneur who perceives an opportunity to innovate may find success dependent upon his ability to hire a visionary entrepreneur (or a team thereof) whose talents, motivations, and interest match those of the proposed innovation. Thus, although varying in emphasis depending upon which stage the firm is in, a cross-fertilization between the two classes of entrepreneurs often serves the end-goal of innovating.

This is important to bear in mind throughout the remaining discussion, which focuses upon organizational entrepreneurs and their role in large corporations, and treats creative and organizational entrepreneurs as if they were two discrete and noninteractive entities. In many cases, this is patently not so. Creative entrepreneurs might approach a large U.S. multinational with an idea for an innovation and, buttressed by sympathetic organizational entrepreneurs, go on to innovate in substantial degree. Or an organizational entrepreneur, perceiving an opportunity to innovate but finding the corporation lacks the creative talent or particular orientation (say, in its R&D laboratories), might seek externally for an appropriate creative entrepreneur.

In small, start-up entrepreneurial firms, entrepreneurs *alone* may demonstrate the skill, interest, and drive to perform both visionary and executor functions; but it is difficult to conceive of a case where, in a large U.S. multinational, the visionary entrepreneur can go on to assume the functions of the executor entrepreneur or vice versa. Since the core subject of this book resides with innovation for foreign markets by U.S. multinationals, and since in all circumstances such multinationals *must* rely upon executor entrepreneurs to take an innovation through all stages to commercialization, our focus now shifts to this class of manager.

The number of U.S. multinationals that innovate abroad is likely to increase in the years ahead. From 1969 to 1979, the number of multinationals that innovated abroad for the first time grew significantly. Of the fifteen innovators in the survey, twelve innovated abroad for the first time after 1969. These innovations abroad added new responsibilities and new challenges for managers.[1]

The contrasts between U.S. multinationals with and without foreign innovations suggest several observations about innovation abroad in the future.[2] First, innovating for foreign markets is a manageable business decision. Although managers perceive the first innovation abroad as highly uncertain, as managers gain experience, the perceived uncertainty of foreign innovation declines rapidly. Second, since some managers appear to have mastered the innovation process abroad, managers of other multinationals who see foreign innovation as a way to compete abroad are likely to be encouraged by those successes. Thus, as managers become convinced of the value of innovating abroad, more and more U.S. multinationals will develop new products and processes for foreign markets as competition abroad increases.

Some multinationals will, no doubt, seek alternatives to foreign innovation.[3] Food and tobacco companies are never likely to undertake innovations either domestically or abroad. Others will rely on other alternatives, such as advertising or large-scale capital investments, to maintain foreign market share. Foreign innovation is far from inevitable for all multinationals. "Yes, we have considered innovating abroad," a European vice president for manufacturing of a U.S. chemical company said, "and we will probably consider it again. But our company has opportunities to grow in foreign markets without innovating in them."[4]

Despite the alternatives available to U.S. multinationals, many managers are now recognizing the necessity for innovation abroad; however, many firms lack the necessary resources for innovation, such as a well-defined strategy and the appropriate structural organization.

No doubt, some managers will try to learn how to innovate abroad as quickly as possible. Although managers will discover shortcuts to foreign innovation, there are many obstacles imposed by time and managers' desire for organizational harmony and continuity.[5] These may be difficult to overcome.

Earlier chapters demonstrated that multinationals face three primary obstacles to foreign innovation: (1) strategic impediments; (2) organizational barriers; and (3) lack of information and adequate measurements of performance. Multinationals confronting any one of these three obstacles seem to be blocked from innovating abroad. In the survey of sixty multinationals, managers that considered their companies as having one or more of the three obstacles had not innovated abroad.

In evaluating the difficulty of overcoming one or more of these obstacles, some managers tended to dismiss the option of foreign innovation in the face of the managerial strains and the uncertainties of implementation. They said, "Innovating abroad in theory is a good idea, but implementing brings on too many headaches." Certainly only the most courageous or foolhardy manager would recommend that a fledgling subsidiary undertake a massive R&D program to innovate without the managerial and technical skills that usually come only after years of experience abroad.

Many multinationals, however, are already equipped with many of the necessities for innovating abroad. Indeed, each of the managers of the fifteen multinationals with foreign innovations viewed their companies as having eliminated all of the barriers. Some, such as Monsanto, are already planning innovations in foreign markets. Other multinationals need only to unify their existing organizations. A few guidelines for innovating abroad follow.

Organization for Foreign Innovation

In some cases, total reorganization is needed. As Chapter 3 showed, not all organizational structures appear equally conducive to foreign innovation. For example, foreign innovations occurred most frequently in geographical area structures.

An example from one multinational illustrates how it reorganized for innovating abroad. Seeing a decline in market share as the result of innovations by European competitors, managers of this multinational decided to introduce new products designed particularly for that market. In implementing their decision, they realized the inadequacy of their organizational structure in Western Europe. The multinational had relied on an international division orientation for its overseas operations. Unlike its domestic operations, its foreign subsidiaries lacked many of the essentials to carry out innovation abroad, including the siting of an R&D facility in Western

Europe, as well as the presence of managers experienced in producing innovations.

To facilitate foreign innovation, the managers refashioned the organizational orientation. They switched from an international division to a structure by geographic areas. They broadened a small Western European engineering department into a full-fledged R&D lab. And they rotated experienced key domestic managers to tours of European duty. Even after realigning the organization and reshuffling managers abroad, the company spent four years gaining experience with its new structure before producing its first innovation abroad.

Few managers are likely to consider undertaking such drastic initiatives to facilitate foreign innovation. Unless management foresees ample rewards from foreign innovation, a firm could hardly justify the internal disruption of complete reorganization.

In other cases, however, a complete reorganization may not be needed. Some U.S. multinationals have already developed many of the organizational essentials cited in Chapters 2 and 3 as conducive to producing foreign innovations. Many multinationals have sited R&D labs abroad, meshed marketing and manufacturing departments that cooperate to facilitate technology transfers, and trained managers and technicians to undertake innovations. Multinationals thus can make several organizational changes to bring about the types of organizational characteristics that managers have consistently emphasized in the survey as useful for innovating abroad.

1. *Link the Channels of Communication.* Since the innovation process requires the cooperation of many managers, formal information flows must connect departments within subsidiaries and link subsidiaries to parent firms and other subsidiaries. The author's survey findings showed that managers of subsidiaries with innovations perceived their organizations as indeed having effective channels of communication in place and operating.

2. *Put Departments Under One Roof.* To foster foreign innovation, managers need certain functions and responsibilities to exist under one organizational roof. For example, R&D labs and marketing and manufacturing departments must coordinate tasks under the responsibility of one subsidiary. In the survey, not one single sub-

sidiary had innovated without there being direct access to R&D personnel as well as to managers of other departments.

3. *Identify Innovation Champions.* Some managers champion innovations well; others do not. For foreign innovation to succeed, top managers must effectively deploy managers who are likely to become innovation champions in foreign subsidiaries. In most cases of innovations abroad identified in the survey, managers could identify innovating champions who persistently advocated the new product or process.

Merging Marketing and Technical Skills in Foreign Subsidiaries

The U.S. multinational considering a strategy of proactive innovation abroad is caught in a dilemma that neither changes in organizational structures nor establishment of formalized communications channels alone can eliminate. That dilemma is caused by a divergence of two necessities for innovation. On one hand, foreign subsidiaries with host-country managers are better equipped to identify local market needs and apply technologies to meet those needs than are parent firms in distant, U.S. headquarters. On the other hand, parent firms based far from foreign markets often have precisely the technicians and managers experienced with the innovation process that foreign subsidiaries lack.

Managers of several U.S. multinationals have overcome this dilemma by fusing the technical strengths of the corporate parents with the marketing strengths of the subsidiaries. As one manager of a U.S. multinational explained:

If a division is expected to produce many innovations, we try to fit the person with the job in our promotion and recruiting systems. We want a person to head the division who is willing to commit himself to back one project at the exclusion of another and follow the project through. That is important. One of the things we had to learn before we could innovate in Europe was that the head of a European division had never initiated the innovation of a new product. He didn't know how to begin. He had always borrowed new products that we had developed in the United States to manufacture abroad. We got around the problem and started developing new products in Europe by dividing our European division into two divisions. The former head of the European division still heads the division with older products, but we made a U.S. manager that developed several new products the head of the division that innovates in Europe.[6]

Managers of the fifteen multinationals identified in the survey as successfully innovating abroad cited the following useful approaches to merging the strengths of parent firms and subsidiaries as useful.

1. *Initiate Project Teams.* Project teams drawn from various departments and markets to develop new products or processes provide foreign managers with access to first-hand experience with the innovation process. These teams help to transplant innovative activities from domestic to foreign markets. Team participation trains foreign managers to coordinate departments, to experience the problems and difficulties of innovating, and to acquire skills with innovating without their feeling that their careers are in jeopardy if the innovation fails.

   Managers surveyed report that the nucleus of the team begins with R&D departments in the United States. Foreign technicians initially participate by performing a specific segment of the overall research, but foreign R&D professionals are involved peripherally in every phase of the research.

   When the innovation process begins to require coordination with the marketing and manufacturing functions, U.S. multinationals then recruit foreign managers from various functional departments as appropriate.

   Managers found the team project approach to be effective in teaching foreign-based managers how better to innovate abroad. By participating directly in developing innovations in the United States, these foreign-based managers learn patterns and procedures of innovating that can be applied in markets abroad.

2. *Rotate Managers Abroad.* The success of innovating lies with managers. Transferring the innovation process from the United States to foreign markets often entails transferring personnel. While many managers of multinationals have lived abroad, the majority of those managers has not worked in the mainstream of their corporations' innovation process. These international managers primarily are associated more with mature products or with well-defined staff functions. They are often process engineers, account-

ants, plant managers, or financial executives. Few have the necessary experience with innovations in the United States to be able to implement innovation in foreign subsidiaries.

The emphasis on domestic activities was underscored in the survey particularly for R&D personnel. Managers of twenty-one multinationals stated that R&D professionals of U.S. multinationals seldom leave the premier U.S. labs for smaller, less prestigious labs sited abroad.

Other managers who were key to domestic innovations viewed rotation to a foreign market as a demotion—a step backward in their careers. One U.S. multinational changed this view by transforming duty abroad from a stigma to a privilege. Using the academic concept of a sabbatical, the multinational annually *honored* specific managers with a year abroad to evaluate foreign technologies and research activities. Their sabbatical assignment included working with a foreign subsidiary that was attempting to innovate abroad.

The value of rotating these managers was twofold. First, the transferred domestic managers encouraged innovation abroad by supplementing subsidiaries' experience with their own experience in developing new products and processes. Second, the rotation of domestic managers frequently resulted in reverse transfers of technologies from foreign markets to the United States.

3. *Institute Training Sessions*. Foreign managers frequently have the ideas and the technical abilities to develop new products or processes, but may lack the skills to organize and coordinate the innovation process. What often distinguishes innovators from noninnovators in the author's survey is the ability of subsidiary managers to know which steps to take to develop a new product or process, and in what order. Although a series of training sessions cannot guarantee success with innovating, training sessions facilitate understanding of the innovation process. This understanding of a complex process has helped some inexperienced subsidiary managers to find shortcuts to innovating abroad.

NOTES

1. Raymond Vernon, "The Future," in Charles P. Kindleberger (ed.), *The International Corporation* (Cambridge, Mass.: MIT Press, 1970), pp. 373–400.

2. The material derives from original research presented by the author in the foregoing chapters.

3. For examples of varieties of strategies, see Raymond Vernon and Louis T. Wells, Jr., *Managers in the International Economy,* 3rd ed. (Englewood Cliffs, N.J.: Prentice-Hall, 1976), Chapters 1–3.

4. Author's interview with the manager of a U.S. multinational, proprietary.

5. As U.S. multinationals gain in the actual operating experience that lessens uncertainties abroad, managers should become more willing to assume the risks that are incumbent upon finding and pursuing shortcuts to innovation. For further discussion, see Raymond Vernon and William H. Davidson, "Foreign Production of Technology-Intensive Products by U.S.–based Multinational Enterprises" (Boston: Harvard University Graduate School of Business Paper, no. 79–5, 1979), pp. 1–79. However, bear in mind that all U.S. multinationals encounter various impediments when expanding abroad.

6. Author's interview with the manager of a U.S. multinational, proprietry.

Appendix:
Author's Survey

In 1979, the author mailed questionnaires to 168 U.S. multinationals identified by Raymond Vernon and William H. Davidson as being involved in the production of technology-intensive products in overseas markets.[1] Of these, sixty firms responded. Subsequent follow-on interviews conducted by the author and analysis of results identified fifteen of these as being successful innovators in markets abroad. Section B lists the sixty responding firms and fifteen innovators, and Section C presents the prototype questionnaire. Responses were supplemented by data drawn from Annual Reports and 10K forms.

The author makes no claim that survey responses are representative of the larger sample population; rather, information gleaned from the survey should be viewed as indicative and impressionistic only. First, a firm's decision to respond to the questionnaire may reflect motivations particular to that firm. For instance, firms involved in innovating abroad, eager to support the survey's objectives, might be inclined to respond in greater detail than firms not actively engaged in innovation abroad. Second, the effects of the biases of those persons responding cannot be discounted. Third, the 168-firm base population was itself skewed. Fourth, knowledgeability of respondents likely varies from firm to firm; however, follow-up interviews explored, and results tended to support, the validity of the written responses.

The fifteen U.S. multinationals identified as being innovators abroad each were requested to give two specific examples of recent innovations. Three multinationals cited innovations in two unrelated product lines, reporting a total of four innovations (two from each of the two unrelated product lines). Thus, the sample of specific innovations abroad consists of 36 rather than 30 observations.

Follow-up interviews of managers were conducted with all fifteen of the innovating U.S. multinationals and eighteen of the forty-five noninnovating. In addition to questionnaire respondents, other domestic and foreign-based managers were also interviewed in most cases.

NOTE

1. For a discussion of how this base sample of 168 firms was selected, see Raymond Vernon and William H. Davidson, "Foreign Production of Technology-Intensive Products by U.S.-based Multinational Enterprises," Harvard University Graduate School of Business Paper no. 79–5, Boston, 1979, pp. 82–86.

LIST OF U.S. MULTINATIONALS IN SURVEY

ALCOA
American Can Company

Beatrice Foods Company
Bendix Corporation* (now Allied Corporation)

Cabot Corporation
Caterpillar Tractor Company
Celanese Corporation
Champion Spark Plug Company
Combustion Engineering, Incorporated
Continental Oil Company
Corning Glass Works*

Dana Corporation
Deere & Company*
Dow Chemical Company*
Dresser Industries

E. I. du Pont de Nemours & Company*

*Firms with foreign innovations

Eastman Kodak Company
Esmark, Inc.
EXXON Corporation

Federal-Mogul Corporation
Firestone Tire & Rubber Company*
Ford Motor Company*

General Electric Company
General Motors Corporation*
Gillette Company
Goodyear Tire & Rubber Company*
W. R. Grace & Company*
GTE*
Gulf Oil Corporation

Hercules, Incorporated
Honeywell, Incorporated

IBM*
Ingersoll-Rand Company
International Paper Company
International Telephone & Telegraph Corporations*

Kellogg Company

Lockheed Aircraft Corporation

Merck & Company, Incorporated
Minnesota Mining and Manufacturing Company (3M)*
Monsanto Company

National Distillers & Chemical Corporation
NL Industries

Olin Corporation
Owens-Illinois, Incorporated

PepsiCo., Inc.
Pet Incorporated
Philip Morris Incorporated
Polaroid

Raytheon Company
RCA Corporation
Rockwell International Corporation

Sperry Rand Corporation
Standard Oil Company of California
Stauffer Chemical Company

TRW Incorporated*

Time Incorporated
Timken Company
Union Carbide Corporation
Westinghouse Electric Corporation

Date _____

Company Name _____

Name and Title of Respondent _____

Address _____ Telephone # _____

Total Company Sales in 1984 _____

Percentage of Total Sales from All Foreign Markets: (Please check one)

0-25% ____   26-50% ____   51-75% ____   76-100% ____

Locations and number of manufacturing facilities in foreign markets and years in market measured by the establishment of your first plant in that market to present:

Market	Number of Plants	Years		
Canada	_____	0-5 __	6-10 __	10-15 __
North America other than U.S. & Canada	_____	0-5 __	6-10 __	10-15 __
Central America	_____	0-5 __	6-10 __	10-15 __
South America	_____	0-5 __	6-10 __	10-15 __
Western Europe	_____	0-5 __	6-10 __	10-15 __
Japan	_____	0-5 __	6-10 __	10-15 __
Hong Kong	_____	0-5 __	6-10 __	10-15 __
Other Asian Countries such as India	_____	0-5 __	6-10 __	10-15 __
Africa	_____	0-5 __	6-10 __	10-15 __
Australia	_____	0-5 __	6-10 __	10-15 __
Carribbean	_____	0-5 __	6-10 __	10-15 __
Other	_____	0-5 __	6-10 __	10-15 __

How much was spent on research and development by your company in 1984? _____

Has your company, since 1978, developed, manufactured, and marketed a new product or a new manufacturing process for a foreign market without first manufacturing and marketing the new product or the new process in the U.S.? While the meaning of "new product" is relatively ambiguous, the meaning of "process" is less so. A new process refers to a method of manufacturing not previously used by the firm.

(continued)

Such methods might include designing new equipment to lower costs or developing a new type of material to replace a high cost material in the product. However, minor modifications to products or processes that are considered routine are excluded.

Yes_____   No_____

If yes, new product _____ new process _____ both _____

If there are a large number of new products or processes, please select one, or possibly a few, which you consider most representative of your firm's decisions and methods in introducing new products or processes in foreign markets. For each new product or process that you select, please identify the location at which the following "steps" of innovation took place:

Research and Development _____

        Basic _____

        Applied/Product Design _____

        Engineering/Commercialization _____

Manufacturing _____

Marketing _____

Was the development of the new product or process done inside or outside the company?

        Inside _____   Outside _____

If inside, please explain how it was done:
        Exclusively at the main R&D facility of the parent firm outside the foreign market _____

        Exclusively at the main R&D facility located in or near the foreign market _____

        Joint effort between the parent firm's R&D facility and the R&D facility in the foreign market _____

If outside, was the development by a:
        Supplier _____

        Independent R&D Laboratory _____

        Other (Explain) _____

Briefly explain why development was done outside of firm.

Briefly outline the history of how the company decided to introduce the new product or process in a foreign market. Please include, if possible, how the company recognized the opportunity, who within the organization urged the firm to introduce a new product or process abroad, why the new product(s) or process(es) were important for the company, and the competitive environment within the foreign market. (Please use reverse side of this page if needed.)

Selected Bibliography

Abernathy, William J., and Balaji S. Chakravarthy. "Government Intervention and Innovation in Industry: A Policy Framework." Harvard University Graduate School of Business Paper no. 78–4. Boston, Mass., 1978.

Abernathy, William J., and James M. Utterback. "Innovation and the Evolving Structure of the Firm." Harvard University Graduate School of Business Paper no. 75–18. Boston, Mass., June 1975.

Adler, F. M., and G. C. Hufbauer. *Overseas Manufacturing Investment: The Balance of Payments*. Report prepared for the U.S. Department of Commerce, U.S. Government Printing Office, Washington, D.C., 1968.

Ansoff, H. Igor, and John M. Stewart. "Strategies for a Technology-Based Business." *Harvard Business Review,* November/December 1967, reprint.

Buckley, Peter J., and Mark Casson. "The Optimal Timing of a Foreign Direct Investment." University of Reading, Department of Economics, Working Paper no. 48. Reading, Pa., February 1980.

Bupp, I. C., and J. C. Derian. *Light Water Reactors*. Basic Books, New York, 1978.

Burns, T., and G. M. Stalker. *The Management of Innovation.*, Tavistock Publishing Co., London, 1961.

Chandler, Alfred D., Jr. *Strategy and Structure: Chapters in the History of the American Industrial Enterprise*. MIT Press, Cambridge, Mass., 1962.

Clee, Gilbert H., and Wilbur M. Sachtjen. "Organizing a Worldwide Business." *Harvard Business Review,* November/December 1964, reprint.

Cooper, Arnold C. "R&D Is More Efficient in Small Companies." *Harvard Business Review,* May/June 1964, reprint.

Drucker, Peter F. "The Discipline of Innovation." *Harvard Business Review,* May/June 1985.

Dunning, John H. "Technology Transfer." In *The International Corporation,* edited by Charles P. Kindleberger. MIT Press, Cambridge, Mass., 1970.

————. "Technology, United States Investment, and European Economic Growth." In *The International Corporation,* edited by Charles P. Kindleberger. MIT Press, Cambridge, Mass., 1970.

Estes, R. M. Reprint of speech, September 20, 1979, provided by General Motors Corp.

Fatemi, Nasrullah S., Gail W. Williams, and Tribaut de Sait-Phalle. *Multinational Corporations.* A. S. Barnes and Co., New York, 1975.

Freeman, Christopher. *The Economics of Industrial Innovation.* Penguin Books, Baltimore, 1974.

Galbraith, John Kenneth. *Designing Complex Organizations.* Addison-Wesley Press, Reading, Mass., 1973.

————. *The New Industrial State.* Houghton-Mifflin Co., Boston, 1967.

Gerstenfeld, Arthur. *Innovation: A Study of Technological Policy.* University Press of America, Washington, D.C., 1977.

Graham, E. M. "Oligopolistic Imitation and European Direct Investment in the United States." D. B. A. dissertation, Harvard University Graduate School of Business, Boston, 1974.

Gruber, William H., Dileep Mehta, and Raymond Vernon. "The R&D Factor in International Trade and International Investment in U.S. Industries." *The Product Life Cycle and International Trade.* Edited by Louis T. Wells. Harvard University Graduate School of Business Administration, Division of Research, Boston, 1972.

Hayes, Robert H., and William J. Abernathy. "Managing Our Way to Economic Decline." *Harvard Business Review,* July/August 1980.

Hirsch, S. *Location of Industry and International Competitiveness.* Clarendon Press, Oxford, England, 1967.

Hymer, Stephen, and Robert Rowthorn. "Multinational Corporations and International Oligopoly: The Non-American Challenge." In *The International Corporation,* edited by Charles P. Kindleberger. MIT Press, Cambridge, Mass., 1970.

ITT, *Annual Report,* 1979.

ITT, "Telecommunications and Economics," pamphlet.

Jewkes, J., D. Sawers, and R. Stillman. *The Sources of Invention.* St. Martin's Press, New York, 1959.

Knickerbocker, F. T. "Oligopolistic Reaction and Multinational Enterprises." D. B. A. dissertation, Harvard University Graduate School of Business, Boston, 1974.

Lorsch, Jay W., and Paul R. Lawrence. "Organizing for Product Innovation." *Harvard Business Review,* January/February 1965.

Mansfield, Edwin. *Industrial Research and Technological Innovation: An Econometric Analysis.* W. W. Norton & Co., New York, 1968.

Markham, Jesse W. "Market Structure, Business Conduct, and Innovation." *American Economic Review,* May 1965.

Mueller, D. C., and J. E. Tilton. "Research and Development Costs as a Barrier to Entry." *Canadian Journal of Economics* 2, no. 4, November 1970.

Myers, M. Scott. "Who Are Your Motivated Workers?" *Harvard Business Review,* January/February 1964.

Nasbeth, L., and G. F. Ray, eds. *The Diffusion of New Industrial Process: An International Study.* Cambridge University Press, Cambridge, England, 1974.

National Science Foundation. *Science Indicators, [various years], Report of the National Science Board, [various years].* U.S. Government Printing Office Stock no. 038–000–00341–1 (for 1977), Washington, D.C., various years.

Nau, H. R. *National Politics and International Technology.* Johns Hopkins University Press, Baltimore, 1974.

Perlmutter, A. "The Torturous Evolution of the Multinational Corporation." *Technological Change and Management.* Edited by David W. Ewing. Harvard University Press, Cambridge, Mass., 1970.

Porter, Michael E. "The Structure Within Industries and Companies' Performance." *Review of Economics and Statistics* 10, May 19, 1970.

Quinn, James Brian. "Technology Transfer by Multinational Companies." *Harvard Business Review,* November/December 1969, reprint.

Robbins, Sidney M., and Robert B. Stobaugh, Jr. *Money in the Multinational Enterprise: A Study in Financial Policy.* Basic Books, New York, 1973.

———. "Some Financial Dilemmas of the Multinational Enterprise." Harvard University Graduate School of Business Administration, original publication series, Boston, 1975.

———. "The Bent Measuring Stick for Foreign Subsidiaries." *Harvard Business Review,* September/October 1978.

Robock, Stephen H. "Political Risk: Identification and Assessment." *Columbia Journal of World Business,* August 1971.

Ronstadt, Robert. *Research and Development Abroad by U.S. Multinationals.* Praeger Publishers, New York, 1977.

Rosenberg, Nathan. "The Direction of Technological Change: Inducement Mechanisms and Focusing Devices." In *Economic Development and Cultural Change* 18, no. 1, pt. 1, October 1969.

Scherer, F. M. *Industrial Market Structure and Economic Performance.* Rand-McNally College Publishing Co., Chicago, 1970.

Schon, Donald A. "Champions for Radical New Inventions." *Harvard Business Review,* March/April 1963, reprint.

———. "Managing Technological Innovation." *Harvard Business Review,* May/June 1969, reprint.

———. *Technology and Change.* Delacorte Press, New York, 1967.

Servan-Schreiber, J. *The American Challenge.* Hamish Hamilton, London, 1968.

Stobaugh, Robert B., Jr. "Competition Encountered by U.S. Companies That Manufacture Abroad." *Journal of International Business Studies,* Spring/Summer 1975.

———. "How to Analyze Foreign Investment Climates." *Harvard Business Review,* September/October 1969.

———. "The Neotechnology Account of International Trade: The Case of Petrochemicals." In *The Product Life Cycle and International Trade,* edited by Louis T. Wells, Jr. Harvard University Graduate School of Business Administration, Division of Research, Boston, 1972.

———. "Where in the World Should We Put That Plant?" *Harvard Business Review,* January/February 1969.

Stobaugh, Robert B., Jr., and Sidney M. Robbins. *Money in the Multinational Enterprise: A Study in Financial Policy.* Basic Books, New York, 1973.

Stobaugh, Robert B., Jr., et al. *Nine Investments Abroad and Their Impact at Home.* Harvard University Graduate School of Business Administration, Division of Research, Boston, 1976.

Vernon, Raymond. "Gone Are the Cashcows of Yesteryear." *Harvard Business Review,* November/December 1980.

———. "International Investment and International Trade in the Product Cycle." *Quarterly Journal of Economics* 80, 1966.

———. "Organization as a Scale Factor in the Growth of Firms." In *Industrial Organization and Economic Development,* edited by J. W. Markham and G. F. Papanek. Houghton-Mifflin Co., Boston, 1970.

———. *Sovereignty at Bay: The Multinational Spread of U.S. Enterprises.* Basic Books, New York, 1971.

————. *Storm Over the Multinationals: The Real Issues.* Harvard University Press, Cambridge, Mass., 1977.

————, ed. *The Economic and Political Consequences of Multinational Enterprise, An Anthology.* Harvard University Graduate School of Business Administration, Division of Research, Boston, 1972.

————. "The Future." In *The International Corporation,* edited by Charles P. Kindleberger. MIT Press, Cambridge, Mass., 1970.

Vernon, Raymond and William H. Davidson. "Foreign Production of Technology-Intensive Products by U.S.–based Multinational Enterprises." Harvard University Graduate School of Business Paper no. 79–5, Boston, 1979.

Vernon, Raymond, and Louis T. Wells, Jr., eds. *Managers in the International Economy,* 3rd ed. Prentice-Hall, Englewood Cliffs, N.J., 1976.

Waltz, Kenneth N. "The Myth of National Interdependence." In *The International Corporation,* edited by Charles P. Kindleberger. MIT Press, Cambridge, Mass., 1970.

Wells, Louis T., Jr. "Negotiating with Third World Governments." *Harvard Business Review,* January/February 1977.

————, ed. *The Product Life Cycle and International Trade.* Harvard University Graduate School of Business Administration, Division of Research, Boston, 1972.

Woodroufe, E. G. "Technology and Business Opportunity for the International Business." *Technological Change and Management.* Edited by David W. Ewing. Harvard University Press, Cambridge, Mass., 1970.

Index

About the Author

FRANK CLAYTON SCHULLER is a Professor at the Amos
Tuck School of Business Administration, Dartmouth College.
Formerly, he was a Research Fellow and Assistant Director of
Special Projects at the Energy and Environmental Policy Cen-
ter of the Kennedy School of Government, Harvard University.
He is the co-editor of *Drawing the Line on Natural Gas Reg-
ulation* (Quorum Books, 1987).